I CAN SEE CLEARLY NOW

by

DeVon White

Prosperity Publishing Solutions Est: 2025

www.prosperitypublishing.net

Other books by DeVon White

Available June 2025: The Harder They Fall

I Can See Clearly Now

Author: DeVon White

ISBN: 9798317675868,

9798317683153, 979-8-3493-9482-9 and

9798317676490

Copyright © 2025 Prosperity Publishing Solutions.

All rights reserved, including the right of reproduction in whole or in part in any form.

Edition: First Prosperity Publishing Solutions Edition

Purchase copies: *I Can See Clearly Now*:
Available online: Barnes & Noble and Amazon

Dedication & Author's Note

By DeVon White

I began writing *I Can See Clearly Now* fifteen years ago. There were moments it felt like it would never see the light of day. But this story refused to stay silent, because it carries the weight of voices that were never meant to be forgotten.

This book is more than fiction. It is a mirror held up to real pain, real systems, and real children whose stories were buried because the world decided they were too inconvenient to hear.

To every voice that has been silenced.
To every truth the world was too afraid to face.
We see you.
We hear you.
We believe you.

This story is for:
The ones still learning how to speak.
The ones who never got the chance.
The ones standing in the rain, waiting for someone to say, *I see you.*

You are not invisible.
You are not forgotten.
Your truth matters.
You matter.

May these pages honor your courage.
May they remember your name.
And may they remind the world what happens when the silenced begin to speak.

Act 1 – Storm Warnings *(Chapters 1–16)*

1. The Storm Knows My Name
2. When Silence Isn't Safe
3. The Ballroom Isn't Big Enough
4. Names the Wind Still Whispers
5. When the City Isn't Loud Enough
6. Where the Trees Still Remember
7. The Quiet That Hears Too Much
8. Things That Don't Exist Anymore
9. Before the Fire Spoke
10. The Price of Printing Truth
11. What the Walls Remember
12. Something Is About to Break
13. The Archive Isn't Closed
14. The Name That Almost Was
15. Some Secrets Still Breathe
16. The Ledger That Wasn't Meant to Survive

Act 2 – The Reckoning *(Chapters 17–30)*

17. The Door That Stayed Shut
18. Where the Fire Was Ordered

19. The People Who Were Watching

20. The Return of Ava Woods

21. The Testimony They Never Buried

22. The Thing She Hid

23. We Remember Her Name

24. The Ones Left Behind

25. Still in Operation

26. The List That Kept Growing

27. The Link They Never Expected

28. A Letter with No Return Address

29. The Man Who Remembered

30. The Mirror Between Us

Act 3 – The Rising *(Chapters 31–44 + Epilogue)*

31. The Trial That Changed Everything

32. The Cross-Examined Silence

33. The Witness That Wasn't Supposed to Speak

34. The Room Where They Waited

35. The Verdict That Burned

36. The Rain That Finally Stopped

37. The Name Beneath the Ash

38. Her Sister's Keeper

39. When the System Apologizes

40. The Garden That Remembers

41. The Wall of Names

42. The Last Time She Spoke

43. The Light We Never Buried

44. A Name for Every Star

Epilogue: The Sky Still Holds Us

I Can See Clearly Now

Act 1 – Chapter 1
Title: "The Storm Knows My Name"

The storm had already swallowed most of the sky by the time Charity Woods reached for her coffee. It loomed over the city like a threat disguised as weather; gray, seething, ancient. Outside the penthouse windows, jagged veins of lightning fractured the clouds. Thunder murmured like a prophecy, and the rain came, soft at first, then sharp as needles.

Charity froze.

The ceramic mug trembled slightly in her hands. She hadn't yet taken a sip. She wouldn't. Not anymore.

Rain never arrived without demanding something in return.

She set the cup down and exhaled, slow and controlled. The morning had started with her usual routine, yoga at 5:30 a.m., almond protein smoothie, a scan of The New York Times. But that had been before the clouds rolled in, before her body began to hum with that strange, vibrating dread she couldn't name. Not fear exactly. Not panic either. Something quieter, deeper. An echo.

From somewhere inside, her heartbeat stumbled.

She turned away from the window and stared at the polished marble floor of her Manhattan penthouse, eyes tracking the trembling reflections of raindrops against the glass. She should be packing. Her flight to Atlanta left in three hours, and the Delta Sigma Theta Founders Gala didn't care about her unresolved grief or unspoken memories. But the storm had rooted her to the floor, one bare foot tucked behind the other, shoulders tense, pulse skipping.

Then came the smell.

Wet wood. Char. Burned paper.

It wasn't real, couldn't be, but the scent was so vivid it wrapped itself around her throat. She closed her eyes, and the air in the room shifted.

Crack!

Thunder rolled across the sky. And just like that, time folded.

She was seven again.

The hallway was filled with smoke. A man's voice was shouting her name, *Charity! Run!* Her hands were pressed to her ears. Her ballerina slippers were wet. Ava was screaming in the distance. The flames hadn't reached her room yet, but the heat had begun to seep through the door frame. She was crying, but no tears came. There was no water. Only fire.

The smell of her mother's perfume; Pleasures for Woman. Her father's cologne, Cool Water. The mirror over her dresser had cracked from the heat. In its shattered surface, she'd seen her own eyes wide with terror, unable to move, locked inside a memory that would later vanish.

Rrring...

This time it was real.

The sound came from her phone, ringing on the kitchen island. She blinked, stumbling out of the trance. Her vision sharpened just enough to make out the caller ID: *Tina Spivey.*

Her sorority big sister. The one who never missed a check-in, especially when galas and memories collided.

Charity grabbed the phone like a lifeline and answered on the second ring.

"Tina."

"Girl, you sound like a ghost. Don't tell me you're backing out again."

"I'm not," Charity said, barely above a whisper.

"You sure? Last year you canceled two hours before boarding. The year before that, you 'forgot' your garment bag. Don't play with me."

"I said I'm coming."

Tina paused. "You alright?"

Charity looked around the kitchen; everything immaculate, sterile. Her hands were still shaking.

"Yeah," she lied.

"Charity."

The silence on the line grew soft with worry.

"Just…weather," Charity said finally. "Storm's messing with my head."

"I figured. It's pouring in Atlanta, too. But the gala's still on. We got new honorees, a jazz quartet, and even Malcolm said he might show up this year. You don't want to miss that."

Charity's lips twitched at the mention of Malcolm. Her steady colleague. The only man in her life who saw through the scaffolding she built around herself and chose to stay anyway.

"I'll be there," she said, more to herself than Tina.

"Good. Your Uber's already en route. I booked it. You have twenty minutes. Don't make me call the concierge like last time."

The line clicked.

Charity placed the phone down slowly, as if it were still smoldering from the call. The sound of rain intensified. It pulsed against the windows in rhythmic bursts, as if knocking to be let in.

She turned to leave the kitchen but stopped at the hallway mirror. It was one of the few reflective surfaces in the apartment she hadn't removed or covered. At least not yet.

Her reflection stared back at her; tall, poised, with a posture so straight it looked brittle. Her black turtleneck and slacks gave her the appearance of invincibility. But her eyes told another story.

She touched the mirror with one fingertip.

In a blink, the reflection changed. The glass rippled. The adult woman vanished, and the child returned.

Little Charity. Hair singed at the ends. Smoke in her lungs. She was holding a pink ballet slipper. Her eyes were wide and red-rimmed.

Charity yanked her hand back.

The image disappeared.

She stumbled toward the bathroom, flipping on the faucet. Cold water. That's what she needed. Something to snap her back.

She splashed her face, but the chill only deepened the fog in her mind.

Behind her, the mirror began to fog. She didn't look at it. Couldn't.

The knock at the door saved her.

A crisp, polite *tap, tap, tap*. It was her kind doorman, informing her of her Uber.

Charity dried her face, grabbed her coat, and moved through the penthouse like a ghost in her own life.

As the elevator descended, she stared at her reflection in the steel doors. Her face was composed again. Presentable. Marketable.

But inside, something was unraveling. The storm hadn't just arrived outside. It had entered her. And it wasn't done speaking.

Act 1 – Chapter 2

Title: "When Silence Isn't Safe"

The ride to the airport unfolded beneath an orchestra of rain.

Charity sat in the backseat of the black SUV, leather interior pristine, her body angled toward the window, though her eyes didn't focus on anything in particular. The driver, a courteous man in his fifties with graying temples and soft jazz humming from the speakers, had offered polite conversation when she entered. She declined with a gentle shake of her head. He hadn't pressed.

She preferred it that way, silence. But even silence could be deceptive. Stillness often made room for what she worked hardest to suppress.

The windshield wipers moved in slow arcs, slicing through memory like the metronome of time. Outside, New York blurred into gray. Inside, Charity counted her breaths and tried not to let the rhythm of the rain carry her backward again.

But it always did.

She hadn't wanted to attend the gala. She never did. The idea of being celebrated made her uneasy, like someone decorating the exterior of a building that was structurally unsound. Still, Tina had a way of pulling her into moments she'd otherwise avoid, and deep down, Charity knew it was time.

Time to stop running. Time to remember why her foundation, The Crossing, existed.

As the car turned onto the ramp leading to LaGuardia, the first image came; not vivid, but persistent.

A door. Wooden, white, and slightly ajar.

It hovered in her mind's eye like a painting half-remembered. She could hear the creak of its hinges, feel the grain of the wood beneath her palm. There was something behind it. Something she hadn't wanted to see.

She blinked it away just as the car slowed to a stop under the departure awning.

"Here you are, Ms. Woods," the driver said, glancing at her through the rearview mirror.

"Thank you," she replied, her voice steady, practiced. She handed him a tip in an envelope she always kept in her purse; cash, generous, discreet.

He smiled and nodded respectfully. "Safe travels."

Charity stepped into the rain.

Even with the canopy overhead, droplets reached her, a kind of divine insistence. She didn't flinch. Just pulled her trench coat tighter and walked inside the terminal like a woman with no ghosts.

The private lounge was quieter than she expected. Dimly lit. Elegantly furnished. Charity settled into a velvet chair near the window and sipped mint tea. Her assistant, Elise, had upgraded her ticket and coordinated everything down to the type of tea stocked in the lounge.

Charity was grateful. Elise had become something of a second nervous system, anticipating needs before they were voiced.

She pulled out her tablet and reviewed the gala's agenda, though she'd already memorized it.

Her name appeared beneath the evening's keynote: "Charity Woods, Founder of The Crossing, Honoring Invisible Survivors."

The irony didn't escape her.

A woman being honored for advocacy she never wanted to do, for a truth she never asked to live.

She slid the tablet back into her tote and leaned back, closing her eyes just briefly.

And that was when it happened.

The silence shifted. Not in the room, but inside her. As though someone had opened a window in her mind.

The fire crackled louder now.

She was no longer in the lounge. Not entirely.

The room was small, with pale green wallpaper and a ballerina figurine resting on a shelf. Her shelf. She remembered it. Her favorite one, the girl frozen in perpetual arabesque.

But something was wrong. Smoke had begun to creep along the ceiling, slow and sinister. There were voices outside the door.

Ava's voice. Then another, lower, commanding.

"Keep her there. Don't let her out."

The child sat on the floor, knees pulled to her chest, eyes wide. Her small hands trembled as the ballerina figurine toppled from the shelf and shattered.

The sound jolted her.

Charity's eyes flew open in the lounge.

Her tea had cooled. Her hands were gripping the armrests so tightly that her knuckles had paled.

She rose, excusing herself to the private restroom, and locked the door behind her.

There, in front of yet another mirror, she studied her face. The sharp lines. The precise makeup. But something beneath her skin was shifting, like a current threatening the structure.

She removed the pin from her hair and let it fall around her shoulders. Her mother used to do that; say it made her look softer, less like a girl trying to be grown.

"You don't have to be strong all the time, baby," her mother would whisper.

But that was before.

Before a detective's lies and a town's silence.

Before the fire.

Before the truth had been buried beneath bureaucratic reports and polished headstones.

Charity leaned closer to the mirror. Her eyes met her own.

"I remember the door," she whispered.

The words made the room tilt slightly, like something important had shifted into place.

The flight was smooth.

Charity kept her headphones in, though she wasn't listening to music. She watched clouds part beneath the plane like curtains. She made no effort to sleep. Sleep was an invitation to dreams, and dreams were dangerous terrain.

Instead, she reread the speech Elise had prepared. It was elegant, moving, full of statistics, and carefully chosen anecdotes. But it wasn't her.

She deleted it and began to type something else. Slower. Raw. From a place she rarely visited.

"There are two kinds of silence," she typed. "The kind that heals. And the kind that hides. I lived in the second one for most of my life. This foundation exists so that others don't have to."

She paused, fingers hovering over the keys.

"I was told I was too young to remember. That forgetting was a blessing. But forgetting is not healing. Healing is remembering and surviving it."

The words sat on the screen like uncut diamonds. Unpolished. But real.

When the plane landed in Atlanta, she was the last to stand. The speech remained unsent, but it felt closer to something true.

Outside the terminal, the air was warm and thick with Southern nostalgia. Charity inhaled deeply, the scent of pine and wet concrete stirring long-buried memories of summers spent beneath willow trees and porch lights.

A black sedan waited curbside, driver holding a placard: *Ms. C. Woods.*

She stepped into the vehicle with a nod, and they pulled away from the airport, city lights blinking through the rain.

They passed under an overpass where graffiti sprawled in red and black: **"Some truths burn."**

Charity's breath caught.

She didn't believe in coincidences. Not anymore.

She reached into her coat pocket and pulled out the photograph she always traveled with. Worn at the edges, faded with time.

Her father, smiling, arms around Ava and herself.

Her mother: mid-laugh, eyes shining with a kind of joy that seemed impossible now.

The photo was taken weeks before the fire.

Back when she believed in safe homes and bedtime stories.

Before silence became the only language that didn't betray her.

As the car curved through Midtown, Charity caught sight of the ballroom where the gala would be held. It gleamed with golden lights and glass walls; transparency made visible.

How ironic, she thought.

She was about to walk into a room full of well-meaning people who would applaud her resilience without ever knowing what it cost.

And tonight, for the first time, she might actually tell them.

Not the full truth. Not yet.

But a piece of it. The kind that makes a ripple.

The kind that begins to open a door.

Act 1 – Chapter 3

Title: "The Ballroom Isn't Big Enough"

The ballroom shimmered like a dream someone else might want to remember.

Crystal chandeliers hung like jeweled constellations, catching light with every tilt of the ceiling fan's windless blades. The air carried a mixture of lavender, citrus, and wealth, an unspoken fragrance of legacy and curated privilege. Soft jazz floated through the space, trailing behind a string quartet perched near the grand staircase.

Charity stepped through the entrance of the Westin Peachtree Plaza's gilded event hall, her heels barely audible on the marble. She paused beneath the archway, letting the grandeur surround her before moving forward, one careful step at a time.

Every eye in the room seemed to find her.

Not out of suspicion, but admiration. Men nodded. Women offered warm smiles. A few whispered her name like a secret they were proud to know.

Charity Elaine Woods.

The keynote. The honoree. The girl who rose from ashes to become the architect of a bridge no one else had dared to build, The Crossing.

She smiled politely. Graciously. Elegantly.

But inside, her breath felt borrowed.

"Look at you," came a familiar voice.

Tina Spivey emerged from the crowd in a floor-length crimson gown, lips painted to match, hair swept into a high twist that declared she had arrived and would not be ignored.

Charity's smile turned genuine. "You always were the storm before the calm."

"And you always deflect with poetry," Tina said, pulling her into a quick embrace. "You look incredible. Black silk was made for you."

"You always say that."

"Because it's always true."

They stood side by side for a moment, scanning the crowd.

"They're already talking about you," Tina said. "Your foundation's numbers from last quarter just hit the press. Over one thousand minors directly assisted. Thirty-seven court cases influenced. And you, madam, are being hailed as 'a modern oracle of justice.'"

Charity raised an eyebrow. "Sounds dramatic."

"Sounds accurate," Tina countered. "And Malcolm's here, by the way."

Charity's pulse quickened, though she betrayed nothing. "Is he?"

Tina gave her a look. "Don't play innocent. You knew. You always know."

Before Charity could respond, the master of ceremonies took the stage and tapped the microphone.

"Ladies and gentlemen, if I may have your attention."

A hush fell. Conversations tapered into silence. Glasses stopped mid-clink. All eyes shifted toward the podium.

"We welcome you tonight not just to celebrate legacy, but to honor those writing the future. This year's keynote is a woman whose work has not only changed lives but unearthed truths most of us were too afraid to see. Please join me in welcoming Ms. Charity Woods."

The applause came like a wave: powerful, polite, slightly rehearsed.

Charity moved through the crowd, spine straight, hands steady. But each step forward felt like peeling skin from a wound she wasn't ready to expose.

The spotlight found her at the podium.

She adjusted the microphone.

Smiled.

Paused.

Then spoke.

"I've spent most of my adult life believing that silence was strength," she began, voice smooth but grounded. "That the less you said, the more you controlled. That burying a thing made it disappear. But the truth is, silence is not strength. It's just silent."

A ripple moved through the audience.

"I founded The Crossing for those who had no one to believe them. For the children whose stories were dismissed, rewritten, or worse, never spoken. For the survivors who learned to make homes out of shame and courage out of necessity."

She let that sit.

"Invisible pain does not mean imaginary pain. And the systems that allow children to fall through cracks…those cracks aren't accidents. They're engineered."

More silence.

And then, murmurs of approval.

Charity continued.

"I was told I was lucky to forget. That I was blessed not to remember the worst night of my life. But memory has its own agenda. It returns when it's ready and when you're ready to receive it."

A pause.

"I don't share my story tonight to be pitied. Or praised. I share it because truth is contagious. And if one person in this room remembers something they were taught to forget, then this microphone has done more than amplify my voice. It has awakened yours."

When she finished, the room remained still. Breathless.

Then, standing ovation.

Charity stepped back, the applause washing over her like a tide she'd braced for but hadn't expected to feel so…real.

Tina met her near the edge of the stage, eyes glossy. "That was surgical."

"It was honest."

"Same thing."

They both laughed quietly.

"Come on," Tina said. "Let me introduce you to some of the honorees."

As the evening wore on, Charity moved gracefully between clusters of conversation, answering questions, exchanging cards, dodging compliments she didn't quite know how to accept. The room buzzed with admiration.

But then, from across the hall, she saw him.

Malcolm.

Not in a suit, he never liked them, but in a charcoal gray blazer over a deep blue shirt that made his skin look like polished mahogany. His presence wasn't loud. It never had been. But it was constant, calming. Like a lighthouse.

Their eyes met. No performance. Just knowing.

He crossed the room slowly, giving her time to pivot if she chose.

She didn't.

"Ms. Woods," he said, voice low, amused. "Always saving the world."

"Mr. James," she replied, tone light. "Always watching me do it."

They stood there for a moment, two people orbiting each other without touching.

"You were remarkable," he said sincerely. "Not just the speech. You."

"Thank you," she said. "I wasn't sure I could do it."

"I was."

She looked at him then. Really looked.

The man who'd helped her build The Crossing. Who'd never asked for more than what she could give. Who had waited without calling it waiting.

"I remember a door," she whispered.

He didn't flinch. "What door?"

"In my childhood home. I couldn't open it before. But it was in my memory today. It was…smoke behind it. I think Ava was on the other side."

Malcolm's brow furrowed, but gently. "Do you want to talk about it?"

She hesitated. "Not yet."

"I'll be here when you do."

And just like that, the noise of the room faded.

Later, after the gala, Charity stood in her hotel suite, barefoot on the rug, dress unzipped halfway, hair loosed and wild. She looked out the window at the city. Atlanta pulsed below her, so familiar, yet so changed.

The storm had followed her here. Or perhaps, she thought, it had never really left.

She walked to the bathroom and flipped on the light. Steam fogged the mirror as she ran hot water into the sink.

Another flash.

The mirror clouded, and once again she was seven.

She stood before the cracked ballerina figurine. This time, she picked up a shard.

Outside the room, a voice called her name.

Then came a man's voice; *Not yet. She's too young. She won't remember.*

But she did.

She dropped the shard. It clattered against the tile.

The mirror cleared.

Charity leaned forward and whispered: "I'm remembering."

Act 1 – Chapter 4

Title: "Names the Wind Still Whispers"

The Atlanta skyline was beginning to dissolve into early morning haze, soft and silver, when Charity woke with a start.

She hadn't meant to fall asleep. After the gala, she'd intended to journal, maybe even draft the next grant proposal for The Crossing. But sometime between untangling her hair and replaying her speech in her mind, the weight of the day had folded over her, pulling her under.

Now, she sat upright in the hotel bed, heartbeat loud, breath uneven.

She'd been dreaming again.

But this dream hadn't been fire and screams. It had been something quieter. Something worse.

She had seen her mother.

Not in the usual flashes or smells. But fully. Speaking.

In the dream, her mother stood at the edge of their front porch in Shady Grove. The summer air was thick, the cicadas shrill. She was holding a book: one of her poetry anthologies and humming a lullaby that Charity hadn't heard in over two decades.

"Every locked door has a key," her mother said, looking directly at her. "But sometimes, it's hidden in silence."

Charity stared at the wall now, her body tense as if the dream were still happening.

She rose, padded across the room to the small writing desk by the window, and opened her notebook. Her handwriting was neat, trained. She flipped to a blank page.

At the top, she wrote:

"My mother spoke to me. In the dream. And I remembered the porch."

She paused.

Then wrote again.

"She knew about the door."

The door. It had returned, not as terror, but as truth.

This time, she could see more of it. The brass doorknob. The streaks of soot along the frame. A child's handprint, small and dark with ash. And on the other side, muffled voices. Her sister's voice.

"Ava."

She whispered the name aloud. The sound felt fragile in the air, as if it might break.

There was a time Charity didn't allow herself to say Ava's name. She was told there had been no body recovered. That the fire had been too intense. That the system had done all it could.

But Charity had learned to decode systemic language.

"All we could do" usually meant *"all we were willing to uncover."*

Later that morning, Charity met Tina for breakfast in the hotel's sun-drenched atrium café.

Tina was already seated, sipping a cappuccino and reading the Sunday paper with her signature red glasses perched low on her nose.

"You look like you didn't sleep," Tina said, not looking up.

"I didn't," Charity replied, easing into the seat across from her.

"You dreamt?"

Charity nodded. "She spoke to me. My mother."

Tina slowly folded the paper. "And?"

"She said something about a key. And silence. And there was a porch. The one from our house in Shady Grove."

Tina exhaled softly. "That's more than you've remembered in years."

"I know."

There was a moment of stillness between them: Tina's eyes assessing, Charity's fingers curled around the rim of her teacup.

"Charity," Tina began carefully, "have you thought about going back? To Shady Grove?"

The words landed like a stone dropped into water.

"No," Charity said instantly. Too quickly.

Tina didn't push. "You might need to. If the memories are coming this strong…"

"I'm not ready."

"I didn't say today. But maybe soon. Ava's voice showing up in your dreams? That's not random."

Charity looked away. Outside the café's arched windows, a fountain danced in the courtyard. Children threw pennies into it, laughing without consequence.

"I need more time," she said softly.

Tina reached over and touched her hand. "Just don't run from what's chasing you. It always finds another door."

By noon, Charity had checked out of the hotel. Her flight back to New York wasn't until the evening, but she needed space: mental, emotional, spiritual. Atlanta had offered her a mirror, and now she needed distance to absorb what she'd seen in it.

She asked the driver to take her to a place no one knew she visited, Piedmont Park.

It was a quiet kind of ritual. Whenever she was in Atlanta, she made a stop there. Not for nostalgia, but for grounding.

She walked the outer paths, head lowered beneath a wide-brimmed hat, black sunglasses shielding her from the world's gaze. Around her, joggers passed, children fed ducks, couples sipped smoothies under trees. Life moved on, indifferent.

She found her bench near the old sycamore tree overlooking the lake. She sat, arms crossed, heart beating too fast for such a peaceful setting.

Then, slowly, deliberately, she opened the journal again.

This time, she began to write what she remembered: not the polished version, but the jagged truth.

"It was raining that night, too. Not heavily. Just enough to make the leaves whisper. I remember the sound of the drops against the roof, and the way Ava pulled me into her room. She was afraid. She never showed it, but I knew. Something had happened at school. Or maybe at Dad's chambers. She said Mama was packing a bag. There was shouting. I didn't understand. I remember holding my ballet slippers. I had a recital that weekend. I thought they were arguing about that. But it was bigger. Something else. Then...the knock. Loud. Heavy. Not friendly. And the fire came soon after."

Charity closed the book, her hands trembling.

She wasn't imagining these fragments anymore. They were returning, whole and relentless.

Someone had come to the house that night.

And whatever they brought with them: threat, warning, destruction, it hadn't been random.

She stood suddenly, breath short.

The wind shifted. The smell of pine. Smoke. Or maybe just memory playing tricks again.

But as she turned to leave, she saw something that stopped her cold.

Across the walking path stood an older man in a faded green coat. Tall, wiry, with skin like weathered leather. His eyes met hers.

Recognition pierced her.

She didn't know how or why, but something in her body screamed: *He was there.*

She blinked, and he was gone.

Vanished into the crowd of strollers and joggers.

Back in the car, she said nothing.

She simply leaned her head against the window and whispered, "It's starting."

The driver glanced in the rearview mirror. "Pardon, ma'am?"

She looked up. "Nothing. Just... thinking out loud."

But she knew better.

It wasn't nothing.

It was the beginning.

Act 1 – Chapter 5

Title: "When the City Isn't Loud Enough"

By the time Charity's flight descended into New York, the city was cloaked in dusk and drizzle.

The skyline, once a source of solace, now looked unfamiliar, like a stranger she'd known too well once, but hadn't seen in years. Lights blinked across the boroughs, each window a world she could not enter. The rain, soft but persistent, returned with uncanny timing. Another storm. Another warning.

She pulled her trench coat closer around her shoulders and stepped into the chilled evening air.

Elise had arranged for a car to meet her at the private terminal. The driver, courteous and wordless, greeted her with a nod before opening the rear door. She appreciated the silence. Talking would feel like betrayal right now, like explaining a grief that hadn't finished forming.

As the car weaved through Queens and across the East River, Charity stared out the window, her reflection overlaying the blurred world outside. The storm's reflection in the glass mimicked the one in her chest.

She touched her wrist absentmindedly, right where the ballerina charm bracelet used to rest. Her mother had given it to her after her first solo recital. A tiny dancer frozen mid-pirouette. It was lost in the fire. Or maybe taken. Like everything else.

Charity blinked and caught her own eyes in the window's mirrored sheen.

"You're still here," she whispered to herself.

The penthouse was dark when she arrived.

Not because Elise hadn't prepared it, she had. Lights were programmed to warm settings. The air carried hints of sandalwood and fresh linen. The fridge had her favorite pressed juices, the marble island gleamed, and the security system lit green. Everything was pristine.

But the darkness was inside her.

She dropped her bags near the hall tree and walked barefoot to the window. The city stretched below like a living map. Taxis glided through intersections, neon signs hummed through the fog, and her own reflection hovered like a second skin against the glass.

It had followed her back, this feeling.

Atlanta hadn't released her. Shady Grove hadn't either.

Charity turned toward the fireplace, untouched since the day she moved in. The remote rested on the mantel. She picked it up and lit the gas flame with a soft click.

The fire roared quietly.

She stared at it, unmoving.

And suddenly, she was seven again.

The flames were real this time. Not memory. Not a dream.

They licked the walls with vicious speed. Smoke spilled under the door. Ava's voice cried out down the hall, then vanished. The floorboards groaned. Their father's study locked. She remembered banging on it, screaming.

Then…

A man.

A man in a brown overcoat. He lifted her into his arms.

"Don't speak. Don't look back."

She clung to him. He covered her eyes.

"I've got you," he whispered. "I've got you, baby girl."

Then they were outside. Sirens. Red and blue lights dancing across the wet lawn. A woman sobbing. Another man yelling.

The house burned.

Her parents were still inside.

And Ava… Ava was gone.

Charity gasped and stumbled back from the fire.

The present rushed in with a violent thud, air, carpet, silence.

Her hand pressed to her chest.

She had seen the man's face. Not clearly, but enough. The shape of his jaw. A scar beneath his eye.

Not a stranger.

Someone known.

She reached for her notebook, kept on the edge of the piano, and opened it with shaking hands.

"The man who carried me out. He was Black. Maybe late 30s. Brown overcoat. Scar near left eye. He said, 'Don't look back.' I didn't. Until now."

She closed the notebook.

Now she had a face to chase.

The next morning, Charity sat in her office at The Crossing headquarters in SoHo: a clean, modern space lined with glass and reclaimed wood. It was early. No one else had arrived.

Her desk was bare, save for a framed photo of her staff, a fountain pen, and a letter from a twelve-year-old girl named Nia. The child had testified last fall against a foster parent who'd manipulated the system for years.

"Thank you for believing me when no one else did," Nia had written in blocky pencil. *"You made me feel like my voice mattered."*

Charity traced her finger over the signature.

She remembered Nia's first intake session: silent, withdrawn, refusing to make eye contact. Charity had seen herself in the child instantly. The same learned mistrust. The same half-buried scream.

She glanced toward the corner of the office where a painting hung, a minimalist abstract with hues of black, gold, and rust. It was the only piece she hadn't chosen herself. Malcolm had gifted it.

She stood and approached the canvas.

At its center was a single white key.

Floating.

Lost.

Her mother's voice echoed: *"Every locked door has a key. But sometimes it's hidden in silence."*

Charity reached toward the painting, fingertips just grazing the texture.

She needed to open the door. Not metaphorically. The literal one, the locked door in their old home. Her childhood memory had been clear: the door was closed, and something was behind it.

Maybe someone.

Maybe answers.

Maybe Ava.

Later that day, Malcolm entered her office without knocking. He was one of the only people who could.

"You're back," he said, voice low.

"I am."

"I saw the fire in your eyes."

She gave a small laugh, but it didn't quite reach her face. "I think I saw a real one, too."

He looked at her more closely. "Something happened."

"I remembered more. The man who pulled me from the fire. His face. His voice."

Malcolm moved to the chair across from her, resting his elbows on his knees.

"You think he's still alive?"

"I think he was trying to protect me. Which means he knew something. Maybe everything."

"You want to find him."

She nodded.

"And the door?" he asked.

"I need to go back, Malcolm. To Shady Grove."

He didn't hesitate. "Then we go."

Charity looked at him, a lump rising in her throat. "You don't have to."

"I do," he interrupted. "You've been carrying this weight for decades. It's time someone walked with you."

That night, she stood on her penthouse balcony, wind curling through her hair, the storm finally clearing.

She held the notebook in her hands. Pages full of fragments.

But no longer broken.

She turned to the final blank page and wrote:

"The fire was meant to erase us. But it didn't. It failed. I'm still here. Ava, if you're alive, if you ever see this, I'm coming. I remember now."

She closed the book, stared into the city, and whispered the name that never stopped echoing in her soul.

"Ava."

Act 1 – Chapter 6

Title: "Where the Trees Still Remember"

The road to Shady Grove stretched like a ribbon unraveled from memory, twisting, sun-warmed, and deceptive in its silence.

Charity hadn't spoken in over an hour.

She sat in the passenger seat of Malcolm's car, staring out at the Carolina countryside as if the trees themselves might whisper her name. The late afternoon light filtered through the dense canopy, casting golden shadows across the asphalt. Every now and then, they'd pass a mailbox leaning like an old man tired of standing or a rusted sign pointing toward some forgotten church.

She remembered this road.

Not from any recent visit. No, she hadn't returned since the funeral. Even then, it was brief. Mechanical. A child being ushered through protocols she couldn't understand. After that, the state had swept her away. Placed her into a "safer environment," as they called it.

But the earth never forgets the feet that once ran barefoot over it.

And neither do the trees.

"You okay?" Malcolm asked gently.

She nodded, not trusting her voice.

They passed a small general store, its paint peeling, front porch still held up by the prayers of old wood.

Beside it stood a pay phone. Charity blinked. She didn't know they even existed anymore.

The town hadn't changed. It had just stood still, waiting for her.

They arrived just as the sun began to tip westward.

Shady Grove was as small as she remembered, barely two hundred people, maybe fewer now. The welcome sign, once proud and freshly painted, now stood faded and chipped: *"Shady Grove – A Place to Call Home."*

It felt like a lie.

Malcolm slowed the car as they entered the town square. Charity's eyes darted to the storefronts, some still open, others boarded up. Johnson's Pharmacy. Miss Letha's Diner. The old post office. Time hadn't erased these things, only softened their outlines.

"I called ahead," Malcolm said. Spoke with the county clerk. They keep property records at the old courthouse. I figured we'd start there in the morning."

She nodded slowly. "Good. I also need to see the house."

Malcolm looked at her. "Today?"

"Yes. I need to see what's left."

They drove in silence toward the northern edge of town, where the houses grew older, land opened wider, and secrets dug deeper.

Then, there it was.

The Woods residence.

Or what remained.

The house stood like a ghost with bones.

The roof had partially collapsed. Vines choked the porch railing. Windows gaped open like empty eyes. But the door, the white wooden door, was still there.

Charity stepped out of the car slowly, the air thick with summer heat and history. Her heels crunched over gravel, then softened over the overgrown path leading to the front steps.

She paused.

Her fingers grazed the porch rail. Splinters kissed her skin. She didn't flinch.

The boards moaned under her weight as she ascended.

Malcolm stayed at a distance, giving her space.

Charity reached for the front door. It swung open without protest.

Inside, time had collapsed. The wallpaper peeled like skin. Furniture lay broken or burned. The air carried the scent of mildew, ash, and something else, something human.

She stepped over debris, her shoes brushing against fragments of a life that once was.

There, beneath a blackened beam, sat the dresser from her childhood room. Its top drawer was ajar, revealing a singed photo frame.

She reached for it.

The glass was cracked, but behind it, her mother, smiling. Holding both girls in her lap. Her father in the background, mid-laugh.

Charity pressed the photo to her chest.

"I found you," she whispered.

She turned toward the hallway.

The one with the door.

Her breath slowed.

She walked it like a prayer.

The door was still there. White. Scarred. Closed.

She reached for the knob. Her hand trembled.

"Not yet," Malcolm said quietly behind her.

She turned. He stood at the edge of the hallway, his presence calm, grounding.

"Why not?" she asked.

"Because once you open it, things change."

"I need them to."

He held her gaze for a long moment, then nodded once.

She turned back to the door.

Turned the knob.

It resisted at first, then gave.

The hinges groaned open.

The room was small, windowless, scorched at the corners. But the floor held something unexpected: boxes.

Unburned. Intact.

Charity knelt.

The boxes were labeled in her father's handwriting.

"CASE FILES – SHG."
"REDACTED – CLASSIFIED."
"WOODS – PERSONAL."

She opened the last one.

Inside were folders. Journals. Photographs.

One showed a group of men in suits, one of them the sheriff at the time. Another man stood beside him. Charity's breath caught.

The man from her memory.

The one who carried her out.

She held the photo close.

"He knew," she whispered. "My father knew."

That night, she and Malcolm stayed at a bed-and-breakfast on the edge of town. The innkeeper, an elderly woman with eyes like storm clouds, welcomed them without questions. Charity couldn't tell whether she remembered her, or had been told to forget.

In her room, Charity spread the contents of the box across the quilt.

Maps. Letters. Newspaper clippings. Names circled in red. One name appeared again and again.

Detective Reginald Lorne.

She remembered that name.

He was the one who'd closed her family's case. Declared it accidental. Labeled her father's inquiries "paranoid." Sealed the files. Retired months later.

Charity stared at his name.

Then opened her notebook.

"Detective Lorne was involved. Daddy knew. Maybe Ava knew. The door was a vault. I was never meant to open it."

She stared out the window at the trees.

They were still.

But she could feel it now.

Something was moving beneath the surface.

The past wasn't dead.

It had simply been waiting.

Act 1 – Chapter 7

Title: "The Quiet That Hears Too Much"

Morning in Shady Grove crept in gently, the way secrets do, on softened footsteps, wrapped in light that didn't quite reach the corners.

Charity sat at the breakfast table of the bed-and-breakfast, staring down at a cup of tea that had long gone cold. She hadn't touched her food: fluffy eggs, buttery grits, a biscuit that steamed when broken. Malcolm had already eaten and left to meet the county clerk about property and court records. He offered to wait, but she had insisted he go ahead.

She needed to sit with what she'd found in that room.

The files were still in her suitcase, carefully bundled. She'd barely scratched the surface. Her father's handwriting danced in her memory: names, abbreviations, shorthand codes she didn't yet know how to interpret. But one truth was clear, Judge Elijah Woods hadn't just stumbled upon corruption. He had documented it. Tracked it. Prepared to expose it.

And it had cost him everything.

Charity lifted the cup to her lips and took a small sip. Cold. Bitter.

A voice stirred from across the room.

"You look just like your mama when you're thinking hard."

She turned.

An older woman stood in the doorway, broom in hand. Late sixties, perhaps older, with silver coiled tight across her scalp and a gaze that didn't miss much. Her name tag read: *Geraldine*.

"You knew her?" Charity asked softly.

Geraldine smiled, though her eyes didn't.

"Knew her? I used to walk you girls to the library while your mama taught night classes at the college. She always smelled like lavender and ink. Wore her hair tied in a silk scarf with poems printed on it."

Charity's chest tightened.

"You remember Ava?" she asked.

Geraldine's hand paused mid-sweep. "Course I do. Wild little thing. Fast runner. Wouldn't let nobody catch her unless she wanted to."

"And after the fire?"

The broom lowered.

Geraldine walked slowly to the table and sat across from her.

"No one ever really said what happened. We heard different things. Some folks said you both died. Some said you'd been taken upstate. But the house was so bad, the story never settled. And no one dared ask too many questions."

"Why?"

"Because silence was safer, baby. And around here, safety don't come from the law, it comes from who's watching."

Charity looked into the woman's eyes. "Who was watching back then?"

Geraldine hesitated. Then leaned in.

"You ever heard of The Grove Five?"

Charity shook her head.

"Back in the '80s, there were five men, well-dressed, powerful. They weren't always in the same room, but they were always behind the curtain. Sheriff, judge, county commissioner, bank president, and one detective. The last one was the one nobody talked about. Reginald Lorne."

Charity's breath stilled.

"He closed my parents' case."

Geraldine nodded solemnly. "And closed more than that. Foster homes. Arrest records. Land deeds. All tied up in his words. That man could erase a life with ink."

Charity leaned forward. "Did people know what they were doing?"

"Some did. Most didn't want to."

"Why not speak up?"

"Because here, the quiet keeps the lights on. Loud people disappear."

The words sank like stones.

Charity reached for her notebook and flipped to a blank page.

"The Grove Five. Sheriff. Judge. Commissioner. Banker. Detective. Silent power. Daddy must have known. That's why he locked the files away."

Geraldine's voice softened. "You looking to stir it all up again?"

Charity looked up. "I'm looking for the truth."

Geraldine sighed and stood. "Then be ready. The truth isn't dead, but it's been hiding a long time, and it doesn't like company."

Later that day, Malcolm returned with two manila envelopes and a worn expression.

"I had to sign three separate logs to get these," he said, handing them to Charity. "They've been buried so deep in 'archived systems' they weren't even digitized."

She took them, heart already thudding.

One was labeled: Elijah Woods – Judicial Notes (1989-1991).
The other: Lorne, Reginald – Internal Inquiry (Confidential).

Charity opened the second envelope first.

Inside were faded pages: typed reports, notes, a psychological review. She scanned the words quickly.

Lorne had been under internal investigation for excessive force, falsified testimony, and multiple sealed complaints from community members. But each complaint had been dismissed.

"Insufficient evidence."
"Witness retracted."
"Matter resolved internally."

She reached the final page. A note, handwritten. Likely from her father.

"Lorne is the thread. Pull it, and it all unravels."

She closed the folder and sat in silence.

That evening, Charity returned to her childhood home alone.

Malcolm stayed behind to contact a law library in Raleigh. They had agreed to take shifts: someone always watching, someone always digging.

Charity stepped through the warped threshold of the burned-out house again, her phone flashlight casting long shadows across the scorched floor. The air smelled less of ash today and more of earth: moss, wet wood, time.

She found her way back to the secret room.

With gloved hands, she examined more boxes. One folder caught her eye.

"Ava – Counseling Notes."

She opened it slowly.

Inside were drawings. Her sister's handwriting. Pages from a therapist's office, clearly smuggled or photocopied.

"Ava talks about a man who follows her home."
"She says Daddy is worried all the time."
"Mentions someone named R.L. who drives by the school."

Charity's mouth went dry.

Ava had seen it too. Felt the danger before the fire. She'd tried to warn them.

And no one had listened.

She clutched the folder to her chest.

"I see you now," she whispered. "I hear you."

Then she turned her head.

A noise.

Outside.

She quickly extinguished the light.

Footsteps. Crunching glass.

A figure: tall, hooded, crossed the porch. Paused. Then walked away.

Not a neighbor.

Not a coincidence.

Charity waited in the dark until the silence returned.

Then she whispered into the dark house, not out of fear, but defiance.

"You didn't kill the story. You just delayed its author."

She rose, tucked the files into her satchel, and stepped outside into the wind.

The moon was low. The trees were still.

But they knew now, she was back.

And this time, she was going to speak until the silence broke.

Act 1 – Chapter 8

Title: "Things That Don't Exist Anymore"

The courthouse clerk's office in Shady Grove had the distinct smell of linoleum, old paper, and resignation.

Charity stepped into the cramped, fluorescent-lit space just after eight a.m., her satchel pressed to her side. Malcolm was across town meeting a contact at the local paper, an old journalist who'd written a suspiciously brief obituary about her father thirty years ago. They had agreed to divide and cover ground, but she still felt the weight of walking in alone.

The receptionist looked up from her desk, surprised. "Can I help you, ma'am?"

"I'm here to request medical records," Charity said evenly. "My sister was treated by a local child therapist before our home burned down in 1991. Her name was Ava Woods."

The receptionist blinked. "That's over thirty years ago."

"I understand," Charity replied, offering a gentle smile. "I just need any record that confirms she was under care. Therapist's name, notes, appointment logs, anything."

The woman looked uncertain. "Medical records that old might've been transferred or purged."

"Could you check?"

She sighed, rising slowly. "Follow me."

They walked down a narrow hallway filled with beige cabinets, the kind with squeaky metal drawers and manila folders stacked like bricks. Charity's fingers twitched as they passed, she could practically hear the voices buried inside.

The clerk paused at a terminal and began typing.

Charity waited, eyes on a bulletin board tacked with outdated community notices: blood drives, turkey raffles, a "Pie for the Pastor" fundraiser dated three years ago.

The keyboard clicking slowed.

The woman frowned.

Charity stepped closer. "What is it?"

She hesitated, then turned the monitor slightly toward Charity. "There's…nothing."

"What do you mean nothing?"

"I mean the name Ava Woods isn't in our system. Not under mental health records, juvenile case files, or intake referrals. It's like she was never here."

Charity's heart pounded. "That's not possible. She was a patient. There are notes in my father's files. Drawings. Sessions."

The woman gave a sympathetic shrug. "If she was seen by a private therapist, maybe the records weren't archived here."

"Could you check by provider instead? Look up licensed therapists in Shady Grove from 1990 to 1991."

The clerk paused again, typing slowly.

A list populated. Only four names.

Two were deceased.

One had retired and moved out of state.

The last one made Charity's breath hitch.

Dr. Lenore Gaines.

That name was written in the margins of Ava's sketches. She remembered it now, looping cursive letters above Ava's pink crayon drawings.

"I'd like to contact Dr. Gaines," Charity said firmly.

The clerk scribbled a phone number on a Post-it note. "She lives out near Oak Hills. Still sees patients, though not kids anymore. You'll have to call her directly."

Charity folded the note carefully into her notebook.

"Thank you," she said.

But as she turned to leave, something gnawed at her.

No record of Ava.

No billing history.

No trace.

Not even a session log.

It wasn't that her sister's story had been lost.

It had been erased.

The drive to Oak Hills took thirty minutes. The road narrowed into tall pines and winding curves, the kind that dared you to drive slowly and listen to your own breath.

Charity parked in front of a quaint stone cottage with ivy-covered windows and wind chimes that danced in the breeze like tiny voices.

She approached the door, hesitated, then knocked twice.

Footsteps. Then the door creaked open.

Dr. Lenore Gaines stood in the doorway, mid-seventies, white hair pulled back in a braid, sharp eyes that had seen too much.

"Yes?"

"Dr. Gaines?" Charity said. "My name is Charity Woods. You treated my sister Ava over thirty years ago."

The woman stiffened, grip tightening on the edge of the door.

Charity continued, gently. "I found your name in my father's notes. We lived in Shady Grove. There was a fire"

"I remember," Dr. Gaines said, her voice low.

"Then you remember Ava?"

She nodded once. "Come in."

The cottage smelled of cedar and rosemary. Books lined every shelf. A small desk in the corner held an old-fashioned tape recorder and a stack of notebooks.

Dr. Gaines motioned for Charity to sit in a worn armchair across from her own.

"I wasn't sure I'd ever see you," she said, settling in. "Or her."

"Then you do remember Ava."

"Of course I do. That girl drew pictures that could break your heart."

Charity inhaled sharply. "What happened to her?"

Dr. Gaines looked down at her lap. "That's the question, isn't it?"

"I went to the clerk's office this morning. There's no record. No files. No billing. It's like she never existed."

Dr. Gaines nodded solemnly. "They came for the files two days after the fire."

"Who?"

"A man in a dark suit. Said he was from the State Child Services Office. Showed me a badge. Asked for everything I had on Ava Woods. Told me the case had been transferred. That I was not to speak about it again."

"Did you believe him?"

Dr. Gaines looked Charity squarely in the eyes. "No. But I was terrified."

Charity felt the air thin.

"They took everything?"

Dr. Gaines hesitated. Then slowly rose and walked to a cabinet in the corner. She opened it with a key from around her neck and pulled out a battered envelope.

"I kept these," she said, handing it to Charity. "I couldn't let them take everything."

Charity opened it.

Inside—three drawings.

Crayon on lined paper.

One showed a house with black smoke curling from the roof. Two stick figures held hands out front. Another figure stood alone by the tree.

The second drawing was a face, angry eyes, scar on the cheek.

The third was a door.

Closed.

Above it, in shaky letters: *"Don't open."*

Charity's hand trembled.

"She knew," she whispered.

Dr. Gaines returned to her chair. "I tried to tell the authorities. But the man came back a week later. Told me my license would be reviewed. My pension threatened. So, I stayed quiet."

"But why?" Charity asked, voice breaking. "Why would they go to such lengths?"

"Because your father knew things they didn't want uncovered. And Ava... she heard things. Saw things. She was a child, but she wasn't blind."

Charity looked up. "Do you believe she survived?"

Dr. Gaines didn't answer right away.

"I don't know," she said finally. "But if she did, they wouldn't have let her stay in Shady Grove."

"Then where would they have taken her?"

The doctor's eyes grew distant.

"There was a program back then," she said slowly. "State-funded. Run through private intermediaries. Children relocated. Renamed. Sometimes adopted. Other times warehoused."

"Warehoused?" Charity echoed.

"Placed in 'therapeutic boarding schools' that were anything but. Off the record. Off the radar. Funded by grants and signed by men like Reginald Lorne."

Charity's breath caught.

"Do you have any names?"

Dr. Gaines shook her head. "Just memories. And guilt."

Charity reached across the space and touched the woman's hand.

"You did more than most. You kept something alive."

That night, back at the bed-and-breakfast, Charity sat with Malcolm by the firepit in the courtyard. The envelope rested between them.

Malcolm studied the drawings, his brow furrowed.

"She was trying to tell someone," he said. "Even if it was only through pictures."

Charity nodded. "And someone made sure no one listened."

He looked up. "What now?"

Charity stared at the flames, eyes fierce.

"We find the facility. We find the program. And if Ava was taken, if she's still alive, we bring her home."

Malcolm nodded slowly. "You're ready."

Charity looked out into the night, wind rustling through the trees like memory returning.

"No," she said. "I'm necessary."

Act 1 – Chapter 9

Title: "Before the Fire Spoke"

Charity stood in front of the Shady Grove Public Library at 9:00 a.m. sharp, the sky gray and heavy like the town's secrets were hiding just above the clouds, waiting to fall.

The building was squat and unassuming: red brick, green shutters, a chipped wooden sign that read: *"Founded 1926 Knowledge Is the Key."* How ironic, she thought. Keys were everywhere lately. In memories. In dreams. Even in the art that Malcolm had unknowingly hung in her office years before.

She had barely slept.

The drawings Ava made, especially the door with *"Don't open"* scribbled above, played on a loop in her mind. But it wasn't fear that kept her awake. It was focus. A hum beneath her skin. She was getting closer. And whoever didn't want her to open that door should've burned more than the house.

Malcolm emerged from the driver's side and met her at the steps. He carried a leather-bound folder under one arm.

"You sure about this?" he asked.

Charity glanced at the windows of the library: dark, dusty, and still. "I have to be."

They entered together.

Inside, the building smelled of old pages and waxed floors. A woman in her fifties sat at the front desk, startled by the sudden company.

"Morning," she said, forcing a smile. "Y'all just visiting or...?"

Charity stepped forward. "I'm looking for archived local newspapers. Specifically, the *Shady Grove Gazette*, between 1989 and 1991. Do you still have physical copies?"

The woman blinked. "That's an awfully narrow range."

"I'm researching a case."

A beat.

"Well... you're welcome to check the basement archive. We don't get many folks down there. But if you pull anything, bring it upstairs for scanning."

"Thank you."

They descended the narrow staircase together, the wooden steps creaking like they hadn't been walked in years. At the bottom, the air turned colder. The basement was lined with tall filing shelves, rows of labeled boxes, and a long microfilm station covered in a plastic sheet.

Malcolm pulled the light cord. A single bulb flickered overhead.

"This place smells like silence," he muttered.

Charity began scanning labels on the metal drawers.

1991. March – May.
1990. October – December.
1989. County Officials.

She pulled a drawer. Dust puffed out like breath. Inside: stacks of clipped newspaper sheets, yellowed and fragile.

She and Malcolm moved carefully, placing pages on the nearby table.

And then, halfway through a stack labeled "Local Politics: 1990" they found it.

A headline.

"Judge Woods Urges Transparency in County Youth Housing Program."

Charity froze.

She scanned the article.

"Judge Elijah Woods has called for an immediate inquiry into Shady Grove's county-funded therapeutic boarding school contracts. In a public statement made at last Thursday's town council meeting, Woods expressed concern over 'irregularities in funding streams, enrollment practices, and long-term mental health outcomes for wards of the state.' Woods stopped short of naming specific facilities, though sources claim his office has launched a formal audit of placement histories from 1987 to 1990."

There was no follow-up article.

No mention of the audit. No further statements.

"Do you see a story after this?" Charity asked.

Malcolm flipped through the next few folders. "Nothing. It's like they pulled the thread and then someone cut the spool."

She stared at the byline. "James T. Elwell."

"That's the guy I met yesterday," Malcolm said. "Used to write for the Gazette. Retired early. Keeps to himself now."

"Did you tell him who you were working with?"

"No. Just said I was doing some research on old civic programs. Why?"

Charity's voice dropped. "Because someone's been following me."

Malcolm looked up.

"The night I was at the house alone," she continued. "Someone came onto the porch. Didn't knock. Didn't speak. Just watched."

He clenched his jaw. "We need to move faster."

She nodded and carefully folded the article into a folder.

"We're not leaving until we find out what this program was," she said. "Whatever Daddy uncovered—it didn't die in the fire. And neither did Ava."

That afternoon, they drove two towns over to the Department of Family and Protective Services Regional

Office, where government records from the late '80s and early '90s were supposedly archived. Charity had made the appointment under a generic foundation request, not mentioning her name or the nature of her investigation.

They were led to a conference room by a quiet assistant who left them alone with a rolling cart of boxes marked "Reallocated Ward Placement – Confidential."

Charity opened the first file and froze.

A photo.

A girl with wide, intelligent eyes. Skin the same tone as hers. The file was stamped:

NAME: ARIA WESTFIELD
DOB: 10/21/1980
PLACEMENT: New Dawn Therapeutic Academy
ADMISSION: May 1991
REMARKS: No immediate family. Behavioral concerns. Memory loss reported post-trauma. No siblings located.

Charity dropped the file.

"It's her."

Malcolm leaned over her shoulder.

"You're sure?"

"Aria. Ava. It's her. They changed her name."

She read further.

TRANSFER NOTES:
Subject was retrieved from house fire incident, admitted under emergency psychological placement clause. No

official adoption requested. Guardianship assigned to state-affiliated care partner. Subject reclassified under behavioral developmental therapy statutes.

"They institutionalized her," she whispered. "They took her, renamed her, and buried her inside a system built to forget."

Malcolm exhaled slowly. "And now?"

Charity turned the page.

RELEASE DATE: N/A. FILE CLOSED. 1999.
NOTES: *Subject no longer at facility. Records sealed by third-party directive. Originating party: DETECTIVE R. LORNE.*

The page blurred in her hands.

"They never let her leave," she said, her voice trembling.

That evening, Charity and Malcolm returned to the inn in silence.

The sun dipped behind the hills, and with it, the warmth left her face.

In her room, she placed Ava's file beside her father's and sat cross-legged on the floor, the pages spread like puzzle pieces across the rug.

One folder had a truth he died for.

The other held the sister who'd been rewritten into silence.

Charity stared at the name Aria Westfield and imagined what that little girl must have thought, waking in a strange place with no familiar faces, her own name stripped like a badge of guilt.

She opened her notebook.

"They changed her name to Aria. But she's still Ava. I don't care what their records say. I remember her laugh. Her run. Her voice telling me to hide under the bed when Mama and Daddy started shouting that night."

She paused.

Then wrote:

"If she's still alive, I will find her. If they buried her... I will dig her out."

Act 1 – Chapter 10

Title: "The Price of Printing Truth"

The house at the end of Magnolia Lane leaned inward like it was bracing for a confession.

Charity stood on the uneven stone path, eyeing the porch sagging beneath the weight of ivy and time. The shutters clung to rusted hinges, and the mailbox hung open, stuffed with fliers yellowing from neglect. But the front door was closed, and behind it lived the man whose name was stamped on her father's final hope: *James T. Elwell, Journalist, Shady Grove Gazette.*

She hadn't called ahead. She hadn't dared.

Truth moved faster than phones.

Malcolm parked discreetly on the shoulder. "You sure you want to go in alone?"

"Yes."

"He buried the article, Charity."

"Then he can dig it back up."

Malcolm nodded once. "I'll be out here."

Charity approached the porch and knocked twice, firm and composed.

At first, silence.

Then a shuffle. A shadow crossed the cracked glass.

The door creaked open.

A man in his late sixties peered through the gap, face half in shadow. His hair, once sandy blond judging by the faded patches, had surrendered to gray. A pair of thin glasses rested low on his nose. His expression flickered between recognition and caution.

"Yes?"

"My name is Charity Woods."

The man stiffened.

"I believe you wrote about my father, Judge Elijah Woods, in 1990."

His lips parted, but no words came.

Charity held up the faded article. "You ran this. Then never followed up. I want to know why."

He opened the door wider but didn't step aside.

"Are you alone?"

"My colleague is waiting outside."

Elwell studied her for a long beat. Then, finally, he exhaled, stepped back, and gestured her in.

The house smelled of newsprint and whiskey. Shelves sagged under the weight of back issues. Framed clippings hung askew on the walls, ceremonial, hollow.

"Don't get many visitors," he said, closing the door behind her.

"I'm not here for pleasantries," Charity replied. "You published the story about my father's investigation into the youth housing programs. But there were no follow-ups. No editorials. No interviews. Just silence."

Elwell walked slowly to a worn recliner and sat down with a groan. "Because I was told to stop."

"By whom?"

He stared at her. "You know who."

"Say it."

He leaned forward. "Detective Reginald Lorne. And he wasn't alone. Sheriff Coulter. Commissioner Wells. Everyone knew your father was poking around in things that didn't want sunlight. When I ran that first piece, I thought I was helping. Thought I was shining a light. But then I got the knock."

"What did they threaten?"

"Everything." He reached into the side table and pulled out a thin manila envelope. "My job. My pension. My wife's disability care. They said my house would go up in smoke next."

Charity's throat tightened. "And so, you stopped."

"I did."

She didn't look away. "You helped bury my father."

The words landed like a slap. Elwell closed his eyes.

"I did," he whispered. "And I've lived with that every day."

He handed her the envelope.

"I kept the notes. The ones I never submitted. He gave me copies, your father. Said, 'Just in case, Jim. If I don't make it to court next month, you tell the story anyway.' I never did."

Charity opened the envelope with trembling hands.

Inside were three pages of typed notes. Her father's voice echoed in every paragraph; legal citations, coded testimony, cross-referenced facility names. One name was circled twice:

"New Dawn Therapeutic Academy – Blackridge, NC."

At the bottom, handwritten in ink:

"They move children like inventory. Ava saw too much. I believe they're watching the house."

Charity's knees weakened. She lowered herself into the opposite chair.

"He knew they were coming," she said.

Elwell nodded. "He tried to file a federal petition. It vanished on its way to Raleigh. Every judge he contacted recused themselves the next day. Said he was hysterical. Paranoid. Lorne was good at that, making good men look unwell."

Charity looked up. "Do you believe my sister survived?"

"I don't know," Elwell said. "But if she did, she wasn't Charity Woods's sister anymore. They would've erased that part of her."

"She became Aria Westfield."

Elwell blinked. "You found her?"

"Her file. Not her."

He rubbed his face. "Then they'll come for you too."

Charity stood. "Let them."

She turned to leave.

"Miss Woods."

She paused at the door.

"They killed your father for what he knew. Don't let them kill your voice for what you remember."

She stepped out onto the porch, heart pounding.

The wind carried the scent of rain.

Again.

Back at the inn, Charity spread the notes on the bed and circled each facility name. The list stretched across five counties, but only one stood out, New Dawn Therapeutic Academy. Her father had marked it three times.

Malcolm entered quietly. "I spoke with the newspaper's current editor. He didn't know about the piece. It never made the digital archives."

"It was pulled," Charity said. "Or never entered. Elwell gave me his original draft. Daddy's notes confirm it, Ava was being watched before the fire. And New Dawn is where she was taken."

"Is it still active?"

Charity nodded. "Rebranded. Now called 'NDA Behavioral Renewal Center.'"

"Sounds sterile."

"Exactly how they like it."

She circled the name.

"I want to go there. Tomorrow."

Malcolm crossed his arms. "And what's the plan?"

"I'll go in as the head of a youth advocacy foundation. Which I am. I'll ask to tour the facility under a donor outreach initiative. Maybe speak to staff. Check their alumni placement records."

"You think they'll let you?"

"If I'm careful."

"And if Ava's not there?"

Charity met his gaze. "Then someone who knows her will be."

That night, the storm finally came.

It hammered the windows with ferocity, rattling the glass like a forgotten truth demanding entry. Charity sat by the fireplace in the inn's parlor, flames flickering against her skin as she opened her notebook once more.

She wrote:

"The town was not asleep. It was complicit. My father was not paranoid. He was precise. Ava was not lost. She was stolen. And I… I am remembering everything."

A sudden knock at the door startled her.

She rose cautiously.

It was the innkeeper, Geraldine. Her eyes looked older tonight.

"You have a visitor," she said quietly. "Said he's from the regional office. Social Services. Asked for you by name."

Charity's blood chilled.

"Now?"

Geraldine nodded. "He's outside. Waiting in a black car."

Charity peeked through the curtain.

The car idled under the lamplight. A man in a dark trench coat stood beside it, unmoving.

Malcolm stepped into the hallway behind her. "Problem?"

Charity looked at him, voice calm but cold.

"They know I'm close."

Act 1 – Chapter 11

Title: "What the Walls Remember"

The drive to the NDA Behavioral Renewal Center began in mist and ended in silence.

Charity sat in the back of the black sedan Malcolm had rented for the day, her Foundation ID badge clipped neatly to her blazer. The satin lining of her coat felt cold against her skin, though she'd worn it a hundred times before. She clutched the leather folder across her lap, the one labeled "Outreach Partnership Proposal," though the documents inside were less about expansion and more about excavation.

Malcolm sat beside her, his voice quiet.

"They vetted us," he said. "Quick background check this morning. Public profiles, IRS filings, foundation grants. All standard."

Charity kept her gaze fixed on the tree-lined road ahead. "And they let us come?"

"Not only that, someone called back personally. Said they were thrilled to host a woman of your stature."

She didn't blink.

"Of course they are," she murmured. "What better way to protect a lie than by feeding it praise?"

They arrived at the facility just after ten.

A long, private driveway wound through a corridor of sycamore trees, revealing the building slowly, like a secret it was reluctant to share.

The structure was impressive: newly painted brick, white columns, a glass entrance with etched lettering that read *"NDA: Empowering the Future."* Beyond the manicured lawn and camera-mounted gateposts, it looked like a campus brochure come to life.

But Charity's skin prickled the moment she stepped out.

The silence was curated.

Even the wind here whispered differently, like it knew not to disturb what had been buried.

They were greeted in the lobby by a woman named **Mrs. Halford**, the Outreach Coordinator.

Middle-aged, impeccably dressed, every word she spoke came wrapped in polished sincerity.

"Ms. Woods, Mr. James, what a privilege," she said, her handshake firm and dry. "We've followed your foundation's work closely. What you've built is extraordinary."

Charity nodded graciously. "We're honored to be here. We're looking to expand partnerships with institutions that serve vulnerable youth in transitional programs."

"Well, you've come to the right place," Mrs. Halford beamed. "Let me show you, our campus."

They followed her down a pristine hallway. Students were nowhere to be seen. Just rows of closed doors and the scent of lemon-scented polish.

"Our youth are currently in guided morning reflection," she explained. "We keep schedules tight. Structure is key to their recovery."

Charity glanced at the closed doors. She remembered how Ava used to draw doors. Always locked. Always alone.

"And how long do most students remain in the program?" Charity asked.

"Depends on the child," Halford replied smoothly. "We customize for every case. Some stay six months. Others… longer."

Charity kept her face neutral. "And what happens after they leave?"

"Oh, we have a robust alumni placement network," Halford said, leading them into a gleaming conference room. "Many transition into vocational programs, apprenticeships, even college."

"Do you maintain alumni records?"

"We do," Halford said. "Though some older files were purged during our rebranding ten years ago."

Charity nodded. "Understandable."

But her mind was racing.

They rebranded the lie. Then they erased the names.

After a brief presentation, mostly statistics and glossy photos, Halford excused herself to retrieve a junior staffer who could answer more operational questions.

Charity turned to Malcolm. "This place is a mausoleum with a facelift."

"They're not even trying to hide the absence of students."

"They don't need to," she said. "They've already silenced the past."

Just then, the door opened.

And in walked a man.

Late forties. Tall. Slight limp. Pale scar across his neck.

Charity's breath caught before she even registered his name tag: **Supervisor D. Kellam.**

He introduced himself curtly and took a seat across from them.

"You wanted information on program continuity?" he asked.

Charity steadied herself. "Yes. We're researching long-term youth outcomes in closed-campus therapeutic settings."

He narrowed his eyes. "And what exactly are you hoping to find here?"

Malcolm shifted in his seat.

Charity met the man's stare without flinching. "History."

A pause. The air tightened.

"We don't keep visitor records from our former identity," Kellam said flatly. "That would compromise confidentiality."

"I understand," Charity replied. "But I'm not here as a stranger. I believe someone I knew as a child was placed here in 1991. She was seven. Her name was Ava Woods. Renamed Aria Westfield."

Kellam didn't move. Didn't blink.

Then, softly, he said, "You need to leave."

Malcolm straightened. "Excuse me?"

"This visit is over. You're trespassing under false pretense."

Charity stood slowly, fire building beneath her calm.

"She was stolen," she said. "Removed from her family under fabricated trauma codes. I have the documents. The name change. The placement record. And now I have your face."

Kellam's voice dropped. "You have no idea who you're dealing with."

Charity took one step forward. "That's where you're wrong. I know exactly who you are. You're one of the men who helped vanish her."

He rose abruptly and signaled for security.

"Escort them out," he barked. "Now."

Two guards appeared almost instantly, tension thick in their shoulders.

Charity reached into her folder, not for a weapon, but for a copy of Ava's placement file, and placed it on the table.

"She existed," she said. "Whether you acknowledge her or not. And I'm going to find her."

Back outside, the wind had picked up. The trees rustled louder, like they were done keeping secrets.

Charity and Malcolm stood beside the car in stunned silence.

Then Malcolm said, "He recognized the name."

Charity nodded. "And the fear in his eyes said the rest."

They drove in silence for miles.

Finally, Malcolm spoke again. "They're going to come for us."

"They already did," Charity whispered. "That man outside the inn last night? That was the warning. This was the escalation."

"And what now?"

She pulled out her phone and began dialing.

"We go public."

Malcolm raised a brow. "Are you sure?"

"I'm not. But I'm done whispering."

That night, back in her hotel room, Charity opened her laptop and composed an email to **Nora Henderson**, a national investigative journalist and longtime advocate for survivors of government negligence.

Subject line: **Buried Truths – Request for Confidential Meeting**

The message was short.

Dear Ms. Henderson,
My name is Charity Woods. You may be familiar with my foundation, The Crossing. I'm reaching out regarding a matter of public interest, possibly national significance, tied to a decades-old youth relocation program operating under multiple government-funded aliases. I believe my sister was among those taken.
Attached is one name: Ava Woods. Renamed Aria Westfield. Last recorded at New Dawn Therapeutic Academy (now NDA Behavioral Renewal Center) in 1991. I have documents. I have a list of names. I have nothing left to lose.
Are you ready to hear the rest?

She hit send.

Then closed the laptop and looked out over the still darkness of Shady Grove.

"I'm not afraid of what they'll take," she whispered.

"I'm afraid of what happens if I stay silent."

Act 1 – Chapter 12

Title: "Something Is About to Break"

The café was quiet, too quiet for a place in the middle of Atlanta on a Monday afternoon.

But that was exactly why Nora Henderson had chosen it.

She sat near the back corner beneath a flickering Edison bulb, her laptop closed, a leather notebook on the table. Her presence was discreet but unmistakable, natural gray coils tucked beneath a slouch beanie, a long tan coat dusted with road grit, and sharp eyes that scanned every entrance before they blinked.

Charity spotted her instantly and made her way over, her own coat still damp from the morning rain. Malcolm remained in the car, parked discreetly two blocks down, watching their surroundings like a hawk.

"Ms. Henderson," Charity said quietly.

"Nora," she replied, standing to offer a firm but warm handshake. "You made good time."

"I didn't want to give anyone time to interfere."

Nora nodded, gesturing to the seat across from her. "Wise. Once you start talking about what they buried, they start watching. That's how it always begins."

Charity sat down, opened her satchel, and pulled out a file folder bound with ribbon. It had taken her three hours to prepare, copies only. The originals were in a locked safe two states away.

"These are Ava's records," she began. "Original name, new name. Intake dates. Facility transfers. And my father's investigative notes. He was a judge, Elijah Woods."

Nora took the folder and opened it, eyes scanning quickly, then narrowing.

"You know what this is, don't you?" she said quietly.

Charity nodded. "I think so."

"It's not just one facility. It's not just one girl. It's a pattern. A map of sanctioned disappearance."

Charity leaned forward. "And I'm tired of following the map alone."

Nora didn't respond right away. She turned the page.

The sketch of the door from Ava's therapy file sat in the middle, as haunting as it had been the first time Charity saw it.

"Do you know what this looks like to an outsider?" Nora asked.

"Paranoia," Charity said. "Conspiracy. Trauma-induced projection. I know. That's what they said about my father too."

"And yet," Nora said, flipping the page, "it's too detailed to ignore. Too many cross-referenced names. Too many sealed files."

She closed the folder gently.

"This is big."

"I don't want attention," Charity said. "I want Ava. And justice for my parents."

"You might have to choose."

Charity's hands folded in her lap. "Then I choose truth."

They spoke for two hours.

Charity shared everything, her father's hidden archive, the erased records, the man who carried her from the fire. She even described the silent visits. The man in the trench coat outside the inn. The facility supervisor who knew Ava's name without needing to look it up.

Nora took notes sparingly, preferring to listen.

Finally, she asked, "Do you have a safe line of communication?"

Charity nodded. "Encrypted channel. We use it at the foundation for whistleblowers."

"I'll send you credentials tonight," Nora said. "Start uploading scanned copies. I want to get this in front of my legal team before it goes anywhere else."

"You believe me?"

"I've been chasing ghosts for twenty-five years," she said, packing up her notes. "But this, this has fingerprints. This has names."

"And if they try to shut you down?"

Nora smiled grimly. "Then they've forgotten who they're dealing with."

Outside the café, the air had thickened again. The rain was preparing a second act.

Charity stood on the curb, phone pressed to her ear.

"Malcolm, we're done. I'll be there in five."

But before she could move, a dark SUV turned the corner, no plates.

Charity's instincts screamed.

She stepped back into the café quickly.

Nora was still inside, speaking with the barista.

"Trouble?" she asked when she saw Charity's face.

Charity nodded. "SUV. Tinted windows. No plates. Circled twice."

Nora didn't blink. "They're faster than I expected."

She reached into her coat pocket and handed Charity a slim USB drive.

"Backup of what I took. Don't trust the cloud. Don't trust email. Keep that off-grid."

Charity tucked it into her inner jacket pocket. "I thought you said you were ready."

"I am," Nora said. "But so are they."

Back at the hotel, Charity double-locked the door and pulled the blackout curtains tight.

Malcolm sat across from her at the small table, scanning the images she'd captured earlier that week, documents, drawings, letters her father never got to send.

"You trust her?" he asked.

"Yes."

"She won't turn this into a headline before you're ready?"

"She's not here for glory," Charity said. "She's here to expose the machine."

Malcolm nodded. "Then we need to prepare."

"For what?"

"For what happens when they can't discredit you."

Charity exhaled slowly. "They'll come for what I love."

"Then we get ahead of them."

The next day, Nora called with news.

"I ran some of your sister's identifiers through a contact," she said. "Guess what? The name Aria Westfield has been used in four different states. All within childcare, housing, or therapeutic education programs."

Charity gripped the phone. "So, she was moved?"

"Or copied," Nora said. "I don't know if they moved her… or if they used her identity as a shell."

Charity swallowed hard. "You mean she might have become a prototype."

Nora hesitated. "Yes."

Charity closed her eyes.

"Then I have to find the original."

That night, another knock at the door startled her.

But it wasn't danger.

It was **Geraldine**, the innkeeper. Her eyes were wide. Her hands clutched an envelope.

"This came for you," she said softly. "No return address. Just slid under the front door."

Charity took the envelope, heart already racing.

Inside was a photograph.

A teenage girl in a school uniform. Eyes wide. Hair pulled back. Face older, harder, but familiar.

The back of the photo read:

"New Dawn. Class of 1996. A.W."

Charity sat on the edge of the bed, unable to speak.

It was her.

Older. Alive.

Somewhere, somehow, **Ava had survived**.

Act 1 – Chapter 13

Title: "The Girl Who Slept Beside Her"

The photograph didn't leave Charity's hands for hours.

She sat on the edge of the bed at the inn, holding it like it was made of breath instead of paper. Ava's eyes, older, hollowed at the edges, but unmistakably Ava, stared back at her from behind a school gate. The uniform was sharp, the building in the background sterile, shadowed by fences dressed in ivy.

New Dawn, 1996.

Five years after the fire.

She had lived.

And someone wanted Charity to know.

"Why now?" she whispered, brushing her thumb over the initials scrawled on the back: *A.W.*

Ava Woods. Or Aria Westfield.

Maybe both.

Maybe neither.

Malcolm entered quietly, having just returned from meeting with a contact at the local university—an archivist who had agreed to provide access to older private school enrollment records in exchange for a donation from The Crossing.

He saw the photo in her hand and stopped mid-step.

"What is that?"

Charity didn't speak.

She simply turned it toward him.

Malcolm stepped forward slowly, then sat down beside her, eyes locked on the image.

"That's her," he said softly.

"I know."

"And someone wanted you to have this."

"Which means someone's watching. Still."

Malcolm's jaw tightened. "And still choosing to help."

Charity looked down. "She was a teenager here. Seventeen, maybe."

Malcolm nodded. "Which means someone in that facility knew her. Lived with her. Ate meals beside her."

"Maybe even remembers her now."

Charity stood and reached for her notebook.

She flipped to a clean page.

"Find survivors. Class of '96. New Dawn."

She paused. Then added:

"Someone knows who she became."

By noon, they were back in Atlanta. Nora had arranged for a meeting with a former New Dawn employee—someone Charity had only just learned about that morning.

Marina Greene.

A former counselor's aide who had worked at the facility from 1993 to 1997. Quietly dismissed when she filed complaints about "emotional neglect, coercive compliance measures, and irregular medical practices."

According to Nora's research, Marina now ran a small trauma recovery center for women in Decatur.

Charity stepped into the sunlit waiting room of *Grace Reclaimed Wellness* with trembling fingers and an iron will.

A receptionist met them at the desk. "Ms. Woods?"

"Yes."

"She's expecting you. Third door on the left."

Malcolm offered her a nod of quiet encouragement. "I'll wait here."

Charity took a deep breath and walked the hall alone.

When she opened the door, she found a small room with soft yellow walls and mismatched chairs. One held **Marina Greene**, late forties, dark-skinned, dreadlocks threaded with silver, and eyes like she'd survived too much but forgot none of it.

"You look like her," Marina said, standing slowly.

Charity blinked. "You knew?"

"I saw the photo. Nora sent it. And I knew those eyes. But it's more than that. It's the way you stand. The way you look when you're trying not to cry."

Charity's voice trembled. "You knew Ava."

Marina motioned to the chair across from her. "I didn't just know her. I slept on the other side of the wall."

They sat across from each other, silence stretching between them like a third presence.

"She came in under the name Aria," Marina began, voice even but raw. "Didn't talk much. Flinched at certain sounds. Kept her shoes lined up under the bed perfectly every night."

Charity inhaled sharply. "That was Mama's rule."

"She said her real name wasn't Aria," Marina continued. "Said she had another name. But every time she tried to say it, she froze. Like someone was gripping her throat from the inside."

Charity pressed her palm against her chest.

"She was smart. Asked questions she wasn't supposed to. Read late at night with a flashlight hidden in a sock. She could memorize entire chapters after one reading."

"Did she ever talk about the fire?"

Marina nodded slowly. "Once. Right after a thunderstorm. She woke up screaming, soaked in sweat. Said something about a door, and a man who said she had to be quiet or 'they'd find the little one.' I think she meant you."

Charity couldn't hold the tears back then.

She turned her face away. Marina handed her a tissue, gentle and wordless.

"Was she... okay?" Charity whispered. "Did they hurt her?"

Marina paused.

"They didn't beat her. Not physically. But what they did was worse. They made her forget. Bit by bit. Took her name, her memories, her story. Told her she had imagined it all. That the fire was a dream. That her parents never existed."

"They erased her," Charity breathed.

"Yes. But not completely. She fought back in her own way."

"How?"

Marina smiled faintly. "Every week, the girls had to write letters as part of therapy. Most just wrote what they were told. But Aria... Ava... she wrote to someone she called 'C.' Just the initial. Every letter started the same: *If you ever remember me, I'm still here.*"

Charity covered her mouth.

"She remembered me?"

Marina nodded. "Every single week."

After a long silence, Charity asked, "Do you know what happened to her?"

Marina's smile faded. "One day, she was just… gone."

"No explanation?"

"They told us she was transferred. But no paperwork. No goodbye. Just an empty bed."

Charity's voice grew hoarse. "Do you think she's still alive?"

Marina looked at her for a long moment.

"I don't know. But I know this, she never gave up on being found. She believed you would come. Maybe not then. But someday."

Charity wept.

And this time, she didn't try to stop it.

Back at the car, Malcolm opened the door for her.

"Well?"

"She remembered me," Charity said.

Malcolm nodded. "Then she's waiting."

Charity stared out the window as the city blurred by.

"I'm going to read those letters," she whispered. "Every single one."

That night, Marina sent the scanned pages.

Twelve letters.

Each addressed to *C.*

Each ending with the same sentence:

"If you ever remember me, I'm still here."

Charity read the last one aloud, voice cracking.

"I'm writing this because I need you to know I didn't forget. Not you. Not Mama. Not Daddy. They told me I was dreaming. That I invented you. But I know the sound of your laugh. I know how you hide your tears by looking up. I know your ballet shoes were pink with a broken strap. You were real. And I was there. If you ever find this, don't stop looking. I'm still here."

Charity clutched the page to her chest.

And finally said the words she had long been afraid to believe:

"I think she's alive."

Act 1 – Chapter 14

Title: "The Name That Almost Was"

The morning fog rolled over the foothills of Shady Grove like a second skin, brushing low against the treetops, blurring everything in a hush of gray. Charity stood on the porch of the inn with a cup of tea warming her hands, the edges of her heart caught between fragile hope and careful restraint.

She had read Ava's letters three times through the night.

Twelve pages of hidden messages, memories disguised as dreams, drawings of pink slippers and tree swings. Each letter had been signed with the same postscript: *"If you ever remember me, I'm still here."*

Now that she did remember, Charity could no longer sleep. Something within her had been activated, not just broken open but lit. She felt taller this morning, not because of posture but purpose. Ava was somewhere on this same map, and every breath Charity took was drawing them closer together.

Her phone vibrated on the railing beside her.

Nora Henderson.

Charity answered on the first ring.

"Say it's good," she said.

Nora didn't waste time. "I think we've found her."

Charity set the cup down with trembling hands. "Tell me."

"A woman in Durham, North Carolina. Volunteers with a trauma recovery program under the name Ria Fields. Early forties. Reserved. Keeps to herself. But here's the part that stopped me cold, she used to go by Aria Westfield."

Charity froze.

"She changed her name five years ago," Nora continued, "dropped the surname quietly and adopted a completely new identity. There's no social media. No driver's license under her former name. The paper trail stops cold."

"But the initials match."

"Exactly. Ria Fields. A.W. Aria Westfield. Too close to be random. And get this, she listed her next of kin once, in a health screening for a community clinic."

"Who?"

Nora hesitated. "She wrote 'C. Woods.'"

Charity's breath left her like a rush of air knocked from the ribs.

"She remembered."

"She didn't forget any of it," Nora said. "She was waiting."

Charity swallowed. "Where is she now?"

"She volunteers three days a week at a women's shelter. I have the address. Want me to make contact?"

Charity shook her head, though Nora couldn't see it. "No. This one's mine."

The drive to Durham took just under four hours.

Charity rode in silence, the photo of Ava tucked into the inside pocket of her coat, resting against her chest like a heartbeat. She had not told Malcolm the full details. Not yet. He had stayed behind to coordinate next steps with Nora and prepare legal support in case things escalated quickly. Which they would.

She preferred to go alone. If Ava truly had survived, if she was indeed *Ria Fields*, then this moment had to happen without an audience. It was not strategy; it was sacred.

Charity pulled into the gravel lot beside a modest brick building, its sign faded but legible: *"Hopewell Community Refuge: Restoring the Whole Woman."* She sat for a moment before exiting the car, eyes on the front door, breath steadying in her chest.

A row of magnolia trees lined the property's edge, their broad leaves trembling slightly in the wind. The air smelled of laundry soap, wood, and the faint aroma of someone baking cornbread.

Charity approached the reception desk slowly. A young woman looked up, friendly but alert.

"Can I help you?"

"I'm looking for Ria Fields," Charity said.

The receptionist paused. "She's not scheduled to volunteer until this afternoon. Are you a client?"

Charity hesitated. "I'm family."

The woman looked her over, noting the name tag clipped to her blazer, the coat, the eyes.

"I'll let Ms. June know," she said. "Wait here, please."

Charity sat down near the window. The waiting room was quiet, warm. There were books stacked on end tables, faded motivational posters on the walls, and a bulletin board covered in photos of smiling women, some holding keys, others holding babies. Faces that had found restoration.

It occurred to her, for the first time, that Ava might have become one of them. Not a child trapped, but a woman healed. A woman who had survived something monstrous and had chosen to stay in the light anyway.

A door creaked open.

An older woman stepped in, gray hair twisted into a low bun, pearl earrings, no nonsense in her walk.

"You're the one asking about Ria?"

"Yes," Charity said, standing.

"She doesn't do surprises."

"I'm not here to surprise her. I'm here to remember her."

The woman studied Charity's face. "You Charity?"

Her voice cracked. "Yes."

The woman's eyes softened. "Come with me."

She was led down a narrow hall lined with rooms that smelled like safety, faint lavender, lemon oil, clean sheets. They stopped at a room marked *Archives*.

"She's sorting donations," the woman said, then knocked twice.

A voice called out. "Come in."

Charity followed the woman in.

There, kneeling on the floor beside a row of bookshelves, was a woman sorting boxes of donated coats and journals. Her hair was twisted neatly, pulled into a bun at the nape of her neck. Her frame was lean. There was something graceful about the way she moved, even while kneeling, something that reminded Charity of ballet.

The woman turned her head slightly, not all the way.

"Yes?"

Charity stepped forward, voice barely above a whisper.

"Ava."

The woman froze.

The coat in her hand slipped to the floor.

Slowly, she turned around.

Their eyes met.

No words.

Just breath.

Just memory.

Then tears.

Ava rose slowly, trembling, one hand reaching forward as if to confirm Charity was real.

"I thought…" she began, then stopped.

Charity moved closer. "You remembered me."

"I never forgot," Ava whispered.

And then they embraced.

Arms wrapped around a lifetime of separation.

It wasn't a fairytale reunion.

It was better.

It was real.

They sat in the small room for over an hour, neither woman rushing the story. Ava, now *Ria*, explained how she had been taken from the fire, renamed, stripped of her past. The years in New Dawn. The letters they forced her to write that she'd turned into code. The way she clung to the memory of pink ballet shoes and rain on windows.

Charity told her everything: the foundation, the search, the files, their father's notes, the people still trying to bury what happened.

Ava wept softly. "I thought you died in the fire. I stopped believing you made it out."

"I thought the same about you," Charity said. "But some things are stronger than fire."

Ava looked down. "I'm not the same. I don't remember everything. Sometimes I still get lost in my head."

"You don't have to remember all of it," Charity said. "You just have to let me walk with you now."

Ava nodded, reaching for her hand.

"I want to come home."

Act 1 – Chapter 15

Title: "What the Silence Tried to Steal"

The drive back to Atlanta from Durham was unlike any Charity had ever taken. Ava sat beside her in the passenger seat, quiet but present, her fingers resting lightly on her knees, eyes watching the trees slip by like ghosts she had once known.

Neither of them spoke for nearly an hour. There was no awkwardness in the silence; it was reverent. Two sisters, split by time and fire, now breathing the same air again. Every few minutes, Charity glanced over, making sure she wasn't imagining it.

Ava would occasionally glance back. And in those brief exchanges, words weren't needed.

Charity reached across the center console and gently laid her hand over her sister's.

Ava flinched at first, just slightly, then laced their fingers together.

"I was afraid I made you up," Ava said quietly.

Charity squeezed her hand. "I thought you were the dream."

The road curved gently beneath them, the early evening sky settling into a soft lilac. Charity had booked them a private suite at a secure location just outside the city, coordinated by Malcolm and Nora. The reunion had shifted everything. They were no longer chasing shadows. The shadow was now sitting beside her, made flesh and memory, willing to be seen again.

At a red light, Charity spoke. "They know I've been looking. They've tried to scare me, discredit me, even stop me."

Ava nodded. "That sounds right. That's what they do."

"They'll try again."

"I'm not afraid."

Charity looked over, surprised.

"I was afraid when I didn't have a name. When I didn't have a voice. But now I do. And you found me. That makes them the ones who should be afraid."

Later that night, in the privacy of their safe location, Malcolm met them with groceries and updates. Nora had secured the encrypted upload of Ava's records and was preparing the first draft of a public exposé with her legal team. Charity had insisted on control over the release, knowing that timing meant everything.

When Malcolm entered the suite and saw Ava standing by the window, his expression changed.

He had seen Charity cry only once. But tonight, something different passed through his eyes, like reverence mixed with rage.

Ava turned.

"You must be Malcolm."

He nodded. "You must be the miracle."

She smiled gently.

He set the bags down and turned to Charity. "You were right."

"I had to be."

He crossed the room slowly, embracing her without words.

Then turned to Ava. "Whatever you need, whatever helps you feel safe, I'm here."

Ava looked between them, something soft settling into her features. "Safety isn't a place. It's a person."

Malcolm said, "Then you're surrounded."

Over the next two days, the suite transformed into a quiet war room. Nora's team began corroborating every detail from Ava's history: placement records, staff rosters, notes from Dr. Gaines, and Marina's archived letters. They created timelines, pinboards, encrypted drives, and hard-copy backups. Charity stayed up past midnight most nights, organizing boxes of files with Ava beside her, sometimes helping, sometimes just watching.

"Why pink?" Charity asked softly during one of their late-night sorting sessions.

Ava looked up from a page she had been tracing her fingers over.

"Your shoes," she said. "The ballet ones. You left one outside my door the night of the fire. I kept it under my pillow for years. It was the only thing they couldn't take from me. I thought, if I could remember that color, then I could remember you."

Charity pressed a hand over her mouth, the tears hot and sudden.

Ava reached over and held her gently. "You're the reason I never forgot who I was."

The plan was simple. Or at least, as simple as it could be.

Nora would release the first wave of findings to a trusted national outlet, an exposé that revealed the rebranding of therapeutic institutions that had buried children under false diagnoses and silenced court records. Ava's name would not appear immediately. They would lead with documented corruption and systematic erasure, focusing on Judge Elijah Woods's case and his efforts to file a federal inquiry.

Once the story had traction, Ava would speak. Not in front of cameras. Not in a press conference. But in her own words, in her own time, through a carefully recorded interview conducted by Nora, and released under Charity's oversight.

Everything was in motion.

And yet, the threat hadn't disappeared.

On the third morning, as Charity stepped into the hallway to retrieve breakfast left by hotel staff, she noticed a detail that didn't belong.

The food was there. The tray untouched.

But at the edge of the mat, tucked beneath a napkin, was a slip of paper.

No envelope.

No signature.

She picked it up.

The handwriting was tight and deliberate.

"Some things are better left buried. Ava wasn't the first. She won't be the last. Walk away while you still can."

Charity closed her eyes.

They had found them.

She locked the door behind her and pressed her back against it, eyes shut tight, the letter still in her hand. Her fingers trembled, but her breathing slowed.

She had expected this.

But something inside her had changed.

She walked calmly into the living room, where Ava was sipping tea and watching the news with the sound off. Malcolm was on the balcony speaking with Nora's legal counsel.

Charity sat beside her sister and placed the note on the coffee table.

Ava read it. Her jaw clenched.

"I know that handwriting," she said.

Charity looked over. "You do?"

Ava nodded slowly. "He worked in records. Back at New Dawn. His name was Donald Cray. Always wore gloves. Had this slow way of talking, like every word cost him a dollar. He watched me. But he never spoke. Not until the day they took me from the facility. He slipped me a piece of paper."

"What did it say?"

Ava's voice dropped. "Your name."

Charity's eyes widened. "You're sure?"

"I still have it. In a book at the shelter. It just said: 'C. Woods. Still alive.'"

Charity leaned back, her heart thudding. "Then this isn't a threat. It's a warning."

"From someone inside."

They both stared at the note again.

"He's telling us something," Ava said. "But he's also afraid."

"We need to find him."

Malcolm entered the room just as they finished speaking.

"We're leaving in two hours," he said. "Nora's team wants to relocate us to D.C. ahead of the release. It'll be safer, and we'll have legal protection if anything escalates."

Charity nodded, then turned to Ava. "Would you be willing to go back? To the shelter, to find that book?"

Ava didn't hesitate. "Yes."

"Then we'll go together."

They arrived in Durham by sunset.

Ava retrieved the book from her old dorm at the shelter: a faded copy of *The Bluest Eye* with pages annotated in blue ink. Tucked inside the back cover was a folded sheet of lined paper.

Charity unfolded it.

"C. Woods. Still alive. Ask for the ledger."

No date. No signature.

Just the note.

Charity whispered the words aloud, her mind turning fast.

"What ledger?"

"I don't know," Ava said. "But someone does."

Act 1 – Chapter 16

Title: "The Ledger That Wasn't Meant to Survive"

The old courthouse in Blackridge, North Carolina, sat beneath the shadows of pecan trees that had stood longer than the building itself. Its red brick exterior had faded under decades of storms and sun, but its bones remained intact, solid as denial.

Charity stood on the worn steps with Ava at her side. The air was thick with August heat, pressing down like consequence. Behind them, Malcolm waited near the car, his eyes scanning the courthouse square with quiet vigilance.

Ava looked up at the building, her face unreadable. "It looks smaller than I remembered."

"That's what happens," Charity said. "We outgrow the places that held us captive."

Inside, the lobby was dim and too quiet, the kind of place where echoes linger longer than voices. The clerk at the front desk was elderly, half-buried behind a stack of file boxes, and completely uninterested in conversation.

Charity approached with calm precision. "Good morning. We have an appointment to review the inactive juvenile case files from 1990 through 1996. Name on the request is Woods."

The clerk barely looked up. "Records room is in the back. Left at the stairwell, third door."

Charity nodded and turned. Ava followed without hesitation.

They found the door labeled **RESTRICTED** and unlocked it with a key mailed to them the day before, courtesy of a court liaison sympathetic to their cause. The room smelled of dust, linoleum, and old plastic. Shelves lined the walls, filled with boxes marked by years and divisions: *Case Intake Logs, Foster Transfers, Ward Evaluations.*

Ava ran her hand along the metal shelf. "We're looking for something called 'the ledger.' Whatever that means."

Charity walked the aisle, eyes scanning. Then she saw it: a narrow box, older than the rest, unmarked by official codes. Taped shut with brittle masking tape, nearly yellowed to gray.

She pulled it down and laid it on the center table. Ava stood at her shoulder as she peeled back the tape and opened the lid.

Inside were three notebooks, bound in blue linen. No titles.

Charity opened the first one.

Rows of names.

First Name, Last Name, Assigned Alias, New Intake ID, Transfer Facility, Status.

Each line was a rebranding of a child.

Some entries had checkmarks beside them.

Others had red lines drawn through their names.

Ava whispered, "This is it."

Charity turned page after page, eyes scanning, hands trembling.

They found Ava's name quickly.

Woods, Ava – Aria Westfield – ID #40477 – New Dawn Therapeutic Academy – Active

Next to her name, in red ink: **"Modified: 'Ria Fields' – Off Record – Reentry: Community Transition."**

Charity exhaled sharply. "They updated it. Even after she left."

Ava pointed to the next entry.

Foster, Devin – Marcus Lee – ID #41230 – New Dawn – Deceased, 1995

She swallowed. "He was in my dorm. He tried to run away."

They kept reading.

Some children were labeled **Relocated.**
Some were labeled **Noncompliant.**
And some were simply **Removed.**

Charity reached the end of the first book and opened the second.

More names.

Dozens.

Then hundreds.

Ava whispered, "They built a whole economy out of us."

Charity sat down, her hands resting on the open page. "They were numbers to someone. Line items. Contracts. Funding benchmarks."

"And no one ever stopped it," Ava said, her voice thin.

Charity looked at her. "Until now."

They took photos of every page. Nora's team would validate the contents, cross-reference against old FOIA requests, and prepare redacted versions for public release. But Ava's name would stay untouched.

"She's not a number," Charity had said to Nora that night. "She's not a case. She's the reason this story has a face."

Back at the inn, Ava sat on the edge of the bed, silent.

Charity brought her a glass of water and sat across from her.

Ava finally spoke. "I don't remember all of them. Just glimpses. The girl who used to hum to herself when she was scared. The boy who left his shoes at the end of the bed in perfect lines. I wonder if anyone is looking for them."

"Maybe they are," Charity said gently. "Maybe this is how we help them find each other."

Ava looked up. "Do you ever wonder what would've happened if the fire never happened? If we'd grown up together, like we were supposed to?"

"All the time," Charity replied.

"Would I still love mango popsicles?"

"Yes."

"Would you still hate thunderstorms?"

"I don't hate them," Charity said. "I just listen to them differently now."

Ava smiled faintly. "I'm scared."

Charity nodded. "Me too. But fear isn't final."

That night, Nora called.

"We've corroborated twenty-three names from the ledger so far," she said. "Some we've located. Some are still missing. One was just released from a private psychiatric hold last year and doesn't even know her name isn't her own."

"What happens when we release this?" Charity asked.

"Powerful people are going to feel exposed," Nora said. "But they'll have no ground left to stand on. Not with this many names, not with this much evidence."

Charity's voice steadied. "Then release it."

The story broke two days later.

"Buried Children, Buried Truths: How Systems Rebranded Trauma as Treatment."

The article included photos of the ledger (with minor redactions), quotes from Charity and Nora, evidence from Charity's father's files, and most importantly, anonymous excerpts from Ava's letters. Her name was not listed, but her words were heard.

It went viral within twenty-four hours.

There were calls for congressional inquiries. Demands for audits. Survivors began stepping forward, one by one. Names that matched the ledger. Stories that had never been believed. Families who had lost children to the system now reawakened to what had truly happened.

But it didn't come without consequence.

On the third day, a rock shattered the window of the foundation's office in New York. On the fourth, Malcolm received a call from an unlisted number warning him to keep Ava off the record.

And on the fifth, Charity's private phone rang at 3:12 a.m.

She answered in a whisper. "Hello?"

A voice: gravelly, deliberate.

"You opened the wrong door."

Then silence.

Charity stared into the dark.

Ava stirred beside her in the next room.

Charity whispered to herself, "No. I opened the only door that ever mattered."

Act 2 – Chapter 17

Title: "The Story That Still Breathes"

Ava sat in the small recording room at The Crossing's private media center, her hands folded in her lap, her shoulders straight, her eyes locked on the camera like it was a window rather than a lens.

Charity watched from the other side of the soundproof glass, seated beside Nora Henderson and Malcolm. The red light above the camera turned on, signaling that the recording had begun.

Nora's voice came softly through the speakers.

"When you're ready, Ava, tell us what you remember."

Ava took a breath that trembled slightly on the way in but settled on the way out.

"My name was Ava Woods. I was seven years old when my house caught fire. It was not an accident. It was set on purpose. I remember the smell of smoke, the sound of my sister crying in the next room, and a man in a coat telling me to run but not speak. I didn't understand at the time, but I do now."

Her voice steadied.

"My father was a judge. Elijah Woods. He was investigating something: corruption tied to private contracts involving foster children and so-called therapeutic programs. My mother was a professor, a woman who told us stories every night and braided our hair in the morning. They were not just good parents. They were dangerous to people who were used to getting away with everything."

Charity felt her throat close. She had imagined this moment for so long, yet the sound of Ava's voice recounting what they had lost made it all real in a way nothing else had.

Ava continued.

"After the fire, I woke up in a different place, wearing different clothes, with a different name. Aria Westfield. I was told the fire was a dream. That I had no parents. That the memories I had were symptoms of trauma, not facts. They called it a protective narrative."

She looked directly into the camera.

"It was a lie."

She paused, then added, "I wrote letters. Every week. I wrote them to a person I was told didn't exist. 'C. Woods.' My sister. I told myself if I remembered her name, I could remember who I was. And now she's here. And I remember everything."

Nora's voice came again. "Do you want this shared?"

Ava nodded. "Word for word. I want someone to hear this and know that I made it through. That being silenced is not the same as being erased. I want them to know what they did failed."

The interview lasted forty-eight minutes.

Ava's recollections were measured but vivid. She described the routines at New Dawn, the children who disappeared, the man named Donald Cray who always wore gloves and spoke rarely but always looked at her like he knew something. She mentioned Marina Greene, the counselor who tried to protect her, and the moment she was relocated again without explanation.

Nora's team reviewed the footage in real time, creating secure backups and preparing a redacted transcript for legal review.

Charity sat in the hallway outside the room when it was over, her hands clasped tight in her lap, her legs crossed at the ankle like her mother had taught her.

Ava stepped out a few minutes later, her expression calm.

Charity stood.

"You were brilliant," she said.

"I was ready."

They embraced again, tighter this time, as if the bond between them had stitched itself back together with every word Ava had spoken on camera.

That evening, Charity sat alone in her office, reviewing documents that had arrived in a sealed envelope postmarked from Shady Grove.

It had no return address.

Inside was a single case file.

Her father's.

Labeled: **CONFIDENTIAL – Sealed by Order of Regional Enforcement Liaison (REL-042).**

Charity opened it slowly, heart pounding.

The contents were familiar at first: memos about Judge Woods's judicial calendar, internal emails, petitions filed and denied. But then she reached a page she had never seen before.

A typed transcript. A phone call. Dated three weeks before the fire.

Caller: Detective Reginald Lorne
Recipient: Commissioner Henry Wells

"We've got a problem. He's not letting go of this. His daughters have seen too much. We might have to push the timeline."

"And what about the mother?"

"She's not the issue. He is. And the older girl. If they disappear together, it'll make waves. If it looks like an accident, no one will question it."

"And the judge?"

"He dies in the fire."

Charity dropped the paper.

Her heart slammed against her chest.

It hadn't just been orchestrated by Lorne. The order had come from someone higher.

Henry Wells.

Commissioner.

One of the Grove Five.

She reached for her phone and called Malcolm.

He picked up immediately.

"They ordered it," she said. "There's a transcript. Commissioner Wells gave the green light to kill them. My father, my mother, and Ava."

Malcolm's voice was grave. "We can prove it?"

"It's here. On tape."

"I'll call Nora. We'll prepare the next release."

Charity stared at the page.

"No," she said. "Not a release. A confrontation."

The next morning, Charity stood on the steps of the Shady Grove Civic Center, Ava at her side, Malcolm behind her, and a row of journalists in front of her. The story had already gone national, but this was something different. This was personal.

She held up the transcript, laminated and marked.

"My name is Charity Elaine Woods. Thirty years ago, my family was destroyed by a fire that was labeled an accident. That was a lie. This document contains a recorded conversation between a now-retired Commissioner and a detective who worked for the county at that time. They discussed the deliberate murder of my parents. They plotted to eliminate my sister and me."

Gasps rippled through the crowd.

Charity did not flinch.

"They failed. And we are here."

She held Ava's hand and raised it.

"We are not victims. We are evidence. And now, so is everyone else whose name appears in this ledger."

Behind her, Nora stepped forward and began to distribute copies of the verified documents to members of the press.

The first journalist raised a hand.

"What happens next?"

Charity looked him in the eye.

"We expose every name. We reopen every case. And we make sure that no child is ever buried beneath the word 'treatment' again."

That night, Charity sat in her apartment for the first time in weeks. The storm that moved over Manhattan had passed, leaving a thin trail of water across the balcony windows. She poured two glasses of tea and carried one into the guest room, where Ava sat reading on the edge of the bed.

Charity handed her the cup.

"I never thought we'd get this far," she said.

Ava smiled. "We're not done yet."

"No," Charity agreed. "But we've started."

Ava sipped quietly.

"Do you still have nightmares?" she asked.

"Sometimes," Charity said. "But now I dream too."

Act 2 – Chapter 18

Title: "Where the Fire Was Ordered"

The town of Shady Grove had changed little, but Charity saw it with new eyes.

The diner on the corner still had rust along its window frames. The library still sat in the shadow of the chapel steeple. And the courthouse, the one where her father had once stood tall and uncompromising, still presided over the square with quiet arrogance. It no longer intimidated her.

She and Ava walked through the square slowly, Ava's arm looped gently through Charity's, their steps synchronized like dancers from a life that had once been theirs. Behind them, Malcolm kept a discreet distance, allowing them to lead, but close enough if needed. The air was heavy with humidity and memory, and the low hum of cicadas clung to the silence like a chorus refusing to be ignored.

Ava paused near the war memorial and stared at the base of the statue.

"I used to think this town was beautiful," she said softly.

Charity looked at her. "That's because you were."

Ava turned her gaze forward again. "Do you think he'll meet with us?"

"He won't want to. But he will."

Commissioner Henry Wells had returned to Shady Grove after his retirement, choosing to spend his twilight years in the very town he had helped corrupt.

He still maintained a modest office inside the town's historical society building, a stone structure that sat across from the county clerk's office. It had once been a schoolhouse, then a voting center, now just a place for old secrets to gather dust.

Charity approached the receptionist, a young woman with glasses and a shaky smile.

"We're here to see Mr. Wells," Charity said evenly.

"Do you have an appointment?"

"No," she said, setting a sealed folder on the counter. "But he'll want to see this."

The woman hesitated, then picked up the phone.

A long pause.

She nodded and pointed to the staircase behind her. "Second floor. End of the hall."

Charity turned to Ava. "Ready?"

Ava's voice was steady. "I've been ready since I was seven."

They walked the hall slowly. The wooden floors creaked beneath their feet, as if the building itself was warning them to turn back. Charity did not stop. She reached the door marked **Henry A. Wells, Commissioner (Ret.)** and knocked once.

"Come in," came a voice from the other side.

Charity opened the door.

The man who sat behind the desk was older now, thinner, his skin spotted with age and his once-commanding posture slightly hunched. But his eyes were the same. Cold. Controlled. Calculating.

He looked up slowly, saw Charity, then Ava.

And for a moment, his face betrayed the smallest flicker of recognition. Not guilt. Just awareness.

"I was told you had documents to deliver," he said.

"I do," Charity replied, stepping forward and placing the folder on his desk. "But I'm not here to deliver. I'm here to confront."

Wells leaned back in his chair. "I'm retired. I don't answer to you."

"No," she said. "But you will answer to the truth."

She opened the folder and spread the pages out before him: the transcript of the phone call, the ledger, the intake record with Ava's alias, the order to silence Elijah Woods, marked with his name and timestamp.

"I know what you did," Charity said. "And I know why."

Wells did not move.

She continued. "You were afraid. My father got too close to the truth. He uncovered the real budget allocations, the rebranded programs, the forced name changes. And instead of facing justice, you tried to burn it down."

Still, no response.

Ava stepped forward, her voice calm but piercing. "You took everything from us. And you were going to leave me in that place forever."

Wells looked at her. "You were just a child."

"I was a witness," Ava corrected. "That was your mistake."

Wells's face tightened. "You have no proof that I gave any direct order."

"I have the transcript," Charity said. "I have the witness. And I have the strength to say your name out loud. In every courtroom, every news outlet, every publication."

Wells leaned forward, eyes narrowing. "You think people will care about an old case from a small town? You think you can threaten me with history?"

"No," Charity said. "I threaten you with the one thing you cannot destroy: survival. We're still here. That's the problem you didn't plan for."

A long silence filled the room.

Finally, Wells spoke. "What do you want?"

Ava's voice answered first. "An apology."

Wells blinked.

"Not for me," she added. "For them. For Mama. For Daddy."

He looked at her, eyes colder than before. "I don't apologize for decisions that protected the system."

Charity shook her head slowly. "Then the system is what we will burn down next. Not with fire, but with light."

She turned and walked out without another word.

Ava lingered at the door. "I remember your voice. You came to the house once. You stood outside the kitchen window and told someone to hurry."

Wells's face went pale.

Ava's voice dropped. "You looked right at me. And I never forgot."

Then she closed the door.

Outside, the air felt different. Lighter. Sharper.

Malcolm waited by the car, holding the door open as they approached.

"How did it go?" he asked.

"He didn't deny it," Charity said. "He just hid behind the word 'system.'"

Ava looked toward the courthouse. "That's all they ever do. Build walls with language."

"Then we'll tear them down with names," Charity said.

They climbed into the car and pulled away from the square.

Behind them, the courthouse faded into the distance, just another brick building with a decaying plaque.

But the truth had been spoken inside it.

And that changed everything.

Later that night, Charity sat on the balcony of her New York apartment, the city humming below like a sleeping giant. Ava joined her with a blanket and two cups of tea.

They sat in silence for a while, letting the air do the talking.

Finally, Charity spoke. "Do you think they'll ever face real justice?"

Ava took a slow sip. "I think truth is justice. The rest is just delay."

Charity nodded. "I still wish I could have saved them."

"You did," Ava said quietly. "You saved their names. You made sure the world didn't forget who they were."

Charity looked at her. "And you?"

Ava smiled faintly. "You reminded me who I was."

Charity reached for her hand.

And together, they watched the sky shift.

For the first time in years, the storm had passed.

Act 2 – Chapter 19

Title: "The Voice at the Podium"

The ballroom at the Manhattan Grand Civic Center had never been so quiet.

Rows of tables stretched beneath a vaulted ceiling strung with lights like constellations. Nearly four hundred guests filled the space: judges, advocates, survivors, donors, and journalists, all seated in poised anticipation. At the front, beneath a clean white banner that read *"The Crossing: Restoring What Was Stolen,"* stood a podium and two chairs, waiting like stage marks for a scene long rehearsed.

Charity stood backstage with Ava, the program booklet in her hands. Her name was printed beside the words *Keynote Speaker*, but her heart was not focused on the speech. It was focused on the woman standing beside her, her sister, no longer lost.

Ava smoothed the lapel of her navy blazer, then glanced at her reflection in the mirror along the wall. She looked calm, polished. But Charity could see the tension just beneath the surface, the way her fingers tapped against her side, the subtle lift of her shoulders when she breathed.

"You don't have to speak if you're not ready," Charity said softly.

Ava turned toward her. "I do. Not for them. For me."

Charity nodded. "You remember how to breathe through it?"

Ava smiled faintly. "Like ballet. Shoulders down, core steady, eyes forward."

They both laughed quietly.

The event coordinator appeared behind them. "Two minutes."

Charity took Ava's hand, held it between her own.

"Whatever happens out there, I am proud of you."

Ava nodded. "And I remember."

They stepped onto the stage together.

The applause came slowly at first, then gathered into a standing wave. Charity walked to the podium, waited for the silence, then leaned into the microphone.

"Good evening. My name is Charity Woods. And I remember."

A pause. A murmur of recognition.

"Tonight is not just a celebration of what we've built. It is a memorial for what we lost. It is a declaration that no child's identity is disposable. It is a promise that names matter."

She looked down at the crowd, then at Ava, seated at her right.

"Thirty years ago, I survived a fire. My parents did not. My sister was presumed dead. I was told to forget. Told to be grateful that I couldn't remember. But memory has its own clock. And this year, the hour struck."

She lifted a small card from the podium.

"In this folder are the names of one hundred and thirty-six children whose identities were altered in state custody. Some are alive. Some are not. All deserve to be known. Tonight, we begin to read their names back into the world."

She held the card, then paused.

"But before we begin, I want to introduce someone. She has waited far too long to be seen."

She turned to Ava, extending a hand.

Ava rose slowly, her steps steady as she approached the microphone. Charity stepped aside, letting her sister stand alone, her story no longer hidden behind someone else's strength.

Ava faced the crowd.

"My name is Ava Woods," she said. "I was taken, renamed, and hidden. But I was not erased. I am here."

Gasps rippled through the room. Several hands rose to mouths. Tears gathered silently.

Ava continued.

"I was placed in a facility that taught me to forget. I was told I was a number. I was told my memories were dreams. But my sister never stopped remembering. And because of her, I now remember too."

She took a slow breath.

"This is not a speech. It is a return."

She stepped back from the microphone and took Charity's hand again. The audience stood, a second ovation rising around them. It was not loud. It was reverent.

Together, they returned to their seats.

Later, in the reception hall, Ava stood near the edge of the room, speaking with a group of survivors who had traveled from across the country. Charity watched from a distance, her heart full. She was not performing. She was present.

Malcolm approached with two glasses of sparkling cider and handed one to Charity.

"You did it," he said.

"We did it."

He looked toward Ava. "She's not who I expected."

"She's who I hoped for."

Charity took a sip and turned her attention to the press table where Nora was speaking with two journalists. One held a notepad, the other a voice recorder. They looked like people who knew they were standing at the edge of something bigger than a headline.

The rest of the evening unfolded in waves: handshakes, quiet testimonies, tears. A woman approached Charity with a folded photograph. Her brother had gone missing in 1992 from a facility in Georgia. His name matched one in the ledger.

"I just needed to say thank you," the woman said. "You made him real again."

Charity accepted the photo with both hands. "We will help you find him."

At the end of the evening, Charity and Ava returned to the penthouse.

They kicked off their shoes in the entryway and made tea in silence. The apartment felt different now. Not larger, but more lived in. Less a monument to isolation and more a resting place between battles.

They sat on the couch, Ava pulling a blanket over her lap.

"I thought I'd feel more... complete," she said.

Charity looked at her. "You don't?"

"I feel seen. But I don't feel finished."

Charity nodded slowly. "Maybe we never are."

Ava leaned her head on her sister's shoulder.

"Do you ever think about the night of the fire?" she asked.

Charity's hand paused on her mug.

"Sometimes. But it's changing. I used to dream about being trapped. Now I dream about escaping."

"I still remember the man who carried you out."

"So, do I. He had a scar below his left eye. Wore a brown overcoat."

Ava sat up slowly. "Did you ever find him?"

Charity hesitated. "No. But I think he left a trail."

Ava's eyes narrowed. "What kind of trail?"

Charity stood and walked to a locked drawer in her study. She returned with a folder and handed it to Ava.

Inside was a photo of the same man: grainy, black and white, pulled from an old personnel file labeled *WITNESS PROTECTION OPERATIVE – STATUS UNKNOWN.*

Charity said, "I think he saved more than just us."

Ava stared at the photo. "Then maybe our story isn't finished yet."

Charity smiled. "Maybe it's just beginning."

Act 2 – Chapter 20

Title: "The Man in the Brown Overcoat"

The folder lay open across the kitchen island, pages spread like puzzle pieces, and at the center of it all, the photograph remained still.

Ava stared at it without blinking.

"I've seen that face in my dreams," she said. "But I thought it was a memory my mind invented to survive."

Charity looked at her. "It wasn't."

The man in the photograph wore a tired expression. His features were sharp, his skin dark, with a scar running just below his left eye. He looked over his shoulder as though someone had called his name mid-thought. There was a date stamped at the bottom: **May 12, 1992**, along with the notation *Status: Inactive, Relocation Approved.*

"I pulled this from a contact in witness protection who owed me a favor," Charity said. "They couldn't give me a name, but the file included this photo and a list of last known case locations."

Ava gently touched the page. "So, he was real."

"He saved us," Charity said, "and then vanished."

Malcolm entered the room holding two mugs of coffee. "I reached out to Nora's team. They're combing the list of officers assigned to judicial protection between 1989 and 1992, focusing on the Southeast region."

Charity looked at him. "And?"

"So far, three names match the age profile and timeline. Two are deceased. One disappeared after a classified reassignment in 1993."

Ava's voice was quiet. "He didn't disappear. He hid."

Malcolm nodded. "And for good reason."

They all looked back at the photo.

"He knew something," Charity said. "He wasn't just there to pull me out of the fire. He knew who set it. Maybe even tried to stop it."

Ava opened the folder's back pocket and pulled out a sealed envelope that Charity had not yet opened. Inside were case notes from a redacted juvenile security log.

A name caught her attention.

Howard Keene.

Charity read aloud. "Former special investigations liaison. Listed as deceased in 1994. No obituary. No death certificate on file."

Ava whispered the name. "Keene. That sounds familiar."

Charity stood. "Then we follow it."

They drove to Greensboro, where the address associated with Howard Keene had last been registered. It was a modest one-story home in an aging subdivision with cracked sidewalks and rusted mailboxes. The lawn was overgrown, and the blinds were shut.

Charity parked the car across the street and remained still for a moment.

"You think he's in there?" Malcolm asked from the driver's seat.

"I think someone is," Charity replied.

They approached slowly. Charity knocked twice on the weathered front door.

A long pause followed. Then the sound of movement: slow, deliberate.

The door opened two inches. A chain rattled.

An elderly man stood behind it, face partially obscured.

"Yes?" he said.

Charity held up the photograph.

"We're looking for the man in this picture."

The man looked at it for a long time.

"I don't know him," he said.

Ava stepped forward. "You carried me out of a burning house."

The man froze.

A long silence followed.

Then he unlatched the chain and opened the door wider.

"Come in."

The interior smelled faintly of cedar and dust. The living room was lined with old bookshelves and faded maps. There were no photographs. Only one wall held any decoration: a bulletin board filled with newspaper clippings and handwritten notes pinned with surgical precision.

The man gestured to the worn sofa.

"I haven't had visitors in twenty years," he said. "Not ones I wanted."

Charity looked at him closely.

"Are you Howard Keene?"

He nodded.

"You saved us," Ava said.

Keene sat down heavily in the chair across from them. "I tried to save your whole family."

Charity's voice caught. "Why?"

"Because I saw what was happening and couldn't live with it. Your father came to me for help. He had documents, names, recordings. He trusted me."

Ava sat forward. "So, you worked inside the system?"

"I did," Keene said. "And I saw what it cost. They were running a ring under the name of child relocation, funding it through shell contracts, hiding it behind therapeutic language. Your father got close to exposing it. Too close."

Charity pulled out the transcript from her bag. "We found this."

Keene looked at it and nodded. "I heard the call. It confirmed everything. I tried to warn him, but I was too late. The night of the fire, I was watching the house. I saw the car pull up. I ran inside as fast as I could."

"You got me out," Charity said.

"I couldn't get to Ava," he said, his voice rough. "The flames cut me off. I was told you both died. But I suspected they took her."

"They did," Ava whispered. "They erased me."

Keene looked at her with eyes full of sorrow. "I wanted to stop it."

Charity's voice was steady. "You started a resistance, didn't you?"

He nodded. "We tried. A few of us. Caseworkers, clerks, a few junior attorneys. We kept copies of everything we could. We hid names in storage lockers, slipped records to journalists. But it was never enough. They were always one step ahead."

Charity sat back, heart pounding. "You still have records?"

Keene stood and walked to a cabinet. He unlocked it, then pulled out a box and set it on the table.

Inside were folders, tapes, and letters.

"This is what's left."

Charity reached inside and pulled out a tape marked **Woods, E. – Testimony (Unfiled).**

"This is my father's voice," she said.

Keene nodded. "He knew he wouldn't survive. He wanted someone to keep the story alive."

That night, back in New York, Charity sat with headphones on in her study, the room dim except for the desk lamp.

She pressed play.

Her father's voice filled the silence.

"If you're hearing this, I didn't make it to court. Which means they succeeded. But they won't win. Because the truth is louder than any fire. My daughters are the key. They remember, even if they don't know it yet."

Charity closed her eyes as tears slid down her cheeks.

She had carried his name.

Now she would carry his fight.

Act 2 – Chapter 21

Title: "The Testimony They Never Buried"

Charity stood at the wide window of her office at The Crossing, her hands resting lightly against the sill, the early morning light casting long shadows across the floor. Outside, the city pulsed with rhythm, honking horns, hurried footsteps, conversations drifting from corner cafés. But inside, the silence was sharper.

On her desk behind her sat a small recorder, a bundle of printed transcripts, and a sealed envelope addressed to the United States Department of Justice.

Her father's voice still lingered in her ears from the night before.

"The truth is louder than any fire."

She had listened to the full recording three times. Each word was deliberate, spoken not as a last resort, but as a legacy. Elijah Woods had not recorded his testimony in fear. He had done so in faith. In faith that someone, someday, would carry it to the place he had never reached.

And now, it was her.

Ava entered the room without knocking, barefoot and quiet. She wore a gray sweater over loose linen pants, her curls pulled back loosely, her expression calm but focused.

"You didn't sleep," she said.

Charity turned. "Neither did you."

Ava walked to the table, picked up the envelope, and turned it over in her hands.

"This is going to shake everything, isn't it?"

Charity nodded. "We're not just naming a pattern anymore. We're naming people."

"And some of them are still in power."

"That's why we can't wait."

Ava sat on the edge of the desk, looking at her sister with unwavering steadiness.

"Are you ready?"

Charity smiled faintly. "I don't think readiness is the point. I think obedience is."

By 10:00 a.m., Charity stood at the entrance of the U.S. District Courthouse in Washington, D.C., flanked by her legal counsel and representatives from two child advocacy organizations. Ava walked beside her, her presence a symbol of the story's resilience.

The Department of Justice had agreed to a closed-door preliminary hearing, following the release of the initial documents and national attention. It was not a trial, not yet, but it was the first official inquiry into a pattern of abuse that had spanned decades.

Inside, the chamber was stark and cold. At the center sat a panel of five federal officials, attorneys, investigators, and one presiding judge. Each had been briefed. Each had a copy of the initial findings. But none had heard the voice that would change everything.

Charity took her seat, opened her folder, and waited for the signal.

The presiding official, a woman named Judge Willa Norcross, spoke first.

"Ms. Woods, we understand you have evidence relevant to our inquiry. You may begin."

Charity stood, hands steady, voice clear.

"What I am about to share was not written by me. It was recorded by my father, Judge Elijah Woods, three weeks before his death in a house fire that was ruled accidental. It was not."

She pressed play on the recorder.

Her father's voice filled the room.

"My name is Judge Elijah Woods. I have served the bench of Shady Grove County for eleven years. I am recording this because I believe I may not live to testify in person. I have uncovered a coordinated effort to reassign children under state protection into rebranded institutions that operate under false therapeutic pretenses. I have collected documents, signatures, financial transfers, and internal communications that link these operations to regional officials, including Detective Reginald Lorne and Commissioner Henry Wells."

The room remained completely still.

"They are silencing voices. Changing names. Disappearing lives. Including my daughter's."

Charity glanced at Ava, whose face had not moved.

"If anything happens to me, let the record show: this was not an accident. This was a consequence of telling the truth."

The tape ended.

Charity looked at the panel.

"The transcript is authenticated. The date of the recording matches the date of the wire transfer from Commissioner Wells's office to an unregistered consulting firm. That same firm was later linked to the restructuring of the facility where my sister was sent."

One of the officials leaned forward. "You're presenting this as coordinated obstruction of justice, correct?"

"Yes. And more than that. It is abuse, fraud, and targeted retaliation against a federal judge."

Judge Norcross folded her hands. "This is no longer a review. This is a criminal investigation."

By the time the hearing ended, Charity felt the exhaustion settle into her bones. Yet beneath it was something else, something solid.

She and Ava stepped out into the daylight, blinking against the brightness.

Nora waited near the steps, phone in hand.

"You did it," she said quietly. "It's moving forward."

"How fast?" Ava asked.

"Fast enough. A federal task force is being assigned. Subpoenas are being prepared."

Charity exhaled. "They'll try to stop it."

Nora nodded. "But now it's bigger than any of us."

That night, back at the penthouse, Charity stood at the balcony window again, watching as the sky shifted from purple to black. She held a cup of tea, steam curling upward like a question still forming.

Ava joined her, holding the notebook where she had copied the names from the ledger. Dozens of names, now verified, were waiting to be restored.

"I keep wondering what Mama would have said," Ava said softly.

Charity didn't answer right away.

Then she said, "She would have said we were brave. And then reminded us to eat something."

Ava laughed quietly. "Probably both."

They stood in silence for a moment longer.

Then Charity said, "There's something else."

Ava looked at her.

"I want to go back."

"Where?"

"To the house."

Ava froze. "Charity, we've already"

"I need to stand there. Not as a girl who ran. As a woman who remembers."

Ava nodded slowly. "Then I'll go with you."

Act 2 – Chapter 22

Title: "The Thing She Hid"

The house stood where they left it.

Twisted vines clung to the bones of the porch. The roof had collapsed in the far corner, exposing the splintered ribs of the attic. Years of wind, rain, and forgetting had worked their hands across the structure, but even now, it did not look like it had given up. It looked like it had waited.

Charity stepped onto the porch first, testing the boards with her weight. They groaned but held. Behind her, Ava moved slower, her breath shallow, her fingers tracing the edge of the doorway as if reacquainting herself with something sacred.

The air smelled like ash and memory.

Charity turned to her sister. "You all, right?"

Ava nodded. "No. But I'm here."

They crossed the threshold together.

Inside, the living room had collapsed into itself. The mantel still stood, but the wallpaper had peeled back like wounded skin. Their mother's favorite armchair was gone, likely burned through. But the fireplace remained, soot-stained and silent.

Charity walked past the ruin, stepping around broken beams and shards of glass. Her feet remembered the layout even if her eyes had to relearn it. She moved to the hallway and paused at a door that hung slightly ajar.

"Is this" Ava began.

Charity nodded. "The linen closet."

She reached for the handle and opened it slowly.

The shelves were covered in a thick layer of dust, the bottom one splintered from water damage. But something caught her eye. Tucked into the far corner was a box. Small. Wooden. Unburned.

Charity knelt and pulled it out.

"What is it?" Ava asked.

Charity opened the lid.

Inside, wrapped in waxed paper, was a locket, a folded letter, and a narrow ballet slipper. Pink. Frayed at the edge. Just like the ones their mother had bought them every Christmas.

Ava gasped and covered her mouth. "That's mine."

Charity handed it to her carefully.

Beneath the slipper, the letter waited. Charity unfolded it slowly.

My girls,

If you are reading this, then something has gone terribly wrong. I have hidden this here because I know your father's enemies are growing louder, and we cannot outrun them forever. I want you to know that we loved you more than anything. If they come for us, it is not because we did something wrong, it is because we did something right.

Charity, you have always been the light in the room. Ava, you are the wind that never surrenders. Together, you are the storm.

Never forget your names. Never forget each other. You will survive. And you will rebuild.

With all my love,
Mama

Ava dropped to her knees.

Charity sat beside her.

They cried without shame.

This was not grief. This was recognition.

Their mother had known.

She had prepared a message not just for their safety, but for their return. And now, after all this time, they had come back to hear it.

They sat in the remains of the hallway for nearly an hour, reading the letter again and again. Ava held the ballet slipper to her chest like an anchor. Charity folded the letter back into its paper and tucked it safely into her coat.

"She didn't just write this to say goodbye," Ava whispered. "She wrote it, so we'd know how to live."

Charity nodded. "Then we owe her that."

Ava looked around the ruined walls. "Do you think we should tear it down?"

Charity shook her head. "No. I think we rebuild it."

"Here?"

"Exactly here."

Later that night, they returned to their hotel and sat in silence by the fire in the lobby. Malcolm joined them after a brief call with Nora, who had confirmed the federal investigation was moving forward. Several officials had already been placed on administrative leave, and a former staffer from the New Dawn facility had offered to testify under immunity.

"It's moving fast," Malcolm said. "But we need to be ready. If you go public with your mother's letter, it will break hearts. But it will also draw fire."

Charity sipped her tea. "Then let it."

Ava spoke quietly. "I want to read it."

Both Charity and Malcolm turned toward her.

Ava looked up. "At the next summit. I want to read her words. Out loud. So, everyone knows what kind of woman she was."

Charity reached across the table and took her hand. "Then we'll print every word."

That night, Charity lay in bed staring at the ceiling.

She thought of her mother's voice, soft and steady, reading them poems before bed.

She thought of her father, always wearing that tired but proud smile whenever she walked into a room.

And she thought of Ava, curled up beside her on stormy nights, whispering stories to drown out the thunder.

They were gone.

And yet, here they were.

Alive in every breath she took.

She closed her eyes and whispered the last line of the letter again.

"You will survive. And you will rebuild."

Act 2 – Chapter 23

Title: "We Remember Her Name"

The Crossing's second annual national summit opened with the usual polish: a reception of dignitaries and activists, name badges gleaming under crystal chandeliers, laughter echoing against the marble floors of the Liberty Hall Conference Center. But beneath the surface, this year was different.

This year, everyone knew what they had come to hear.

Ava Woods.

Her name was now known. Not as a victim. Not as a missing child. But as a survivor who had outlived the systems meant to erase her. And tonight, for the first time, she would speak not as someone recounting trauma, but as someone reclaiming legacy.

Charity stood at the edge of the ballroom, watching the stage from the wings as technicians made final adjustments. The backdrop was a simple navy velvet curtain, with a white oak lectern centered beneath a soft golden light. There were no slides. No videos. Just a voice, and a letter.

Malcolm approached with a tablet in hand, scrolling through the evening program.

"She's the final speaker," he said. "They're calling it the candlelight address."

Charity smiled. "She's ready."

He glanced at her. "And you?"

She nodded. "Tonight, I stop carrying the burden alone."

At 7:34 p.m., the lights dimmed.

A hush moved through the audience, rippling gently as people settled into their chairs. Charity stepped to the podium first.

"Good evening," she began, her voice steady and sure. "I do not come to close this event. I come to open a door."

She paused.

"You have heard the data. You have seen the faces. You have followed the threads. But tonight, we remember the woman who first knew what was happening. The one who wrote to two little girls on the night of her death, believing one day they might find her words again."

She looked toward the wings.

"My sister found them. And she is here."

The audience rose to their feet as Ava stepped forward slowly, holding a folded sheet of paper pressed to her heart. She wore a deep green dress, simple and graceful, her curls pulled away from her face. She did not wave. She did not bow. She simply took her place behind the podium, waited for the silence, and began to read.

"My girls,"
"If you are reading this, then something has gone terribly wrong. I have hidden this here because I know your father's enemies are growing louder, and we cannot outrun them forever. I want you to know that we loved you more than anything. If they come for us, it is not because we did something wrong. It is because we did something right."

Ava's voice trembled, but she did not stop.

"Charity, you have always been the light in the room. Ava, you are the wind that never surrenders. Together, you are the storm."

People in the audience began to cry quietly, tissues pressed to mouths, hands covering hearts.

"Never forget your names. Never forget each other. You will survive. And you will rebuild."
"With all my love,
Mama"

Ava folded the paper slowly and placed it on the lectern.

Then she spoke without reading.

"My mother's name was Leah Elaine Woods. She taught English literature at a local college. She believed that every story mattered. That no voice should be lost. That every name should be spoken with care. Tonight, I speak hers."

She paused.

"And I ask that you speak the names of those you've lost. Not just the ones who died, but the ones who were taken. Taken by systems, by silence, by shame. Speak them. Write them. Carry them."

She took a slow breath.

"I am here because someone remembered my name. And now, I remember yours."

She stepped back from the podium.

The silence was long.

Then it broke like a wave.

The audience rose again, not in politeness, but in reverence. Many wept openly. Some reached out to touch the shoulder of the person next to them. Others simply stood in place, holding the moment like a fragile glass that could not be dropped.

Charity stepped onto the stage and took her sister's hand.

Together, they stood in the light.

Later that night, Ava and Charity sat on the floor of their hotel suite, their heels discarded, their dresses slightly wrinkled, their tea mugs cooling beside them.

"That was the bravest thing I've ever seen," Charity said softly.

Ava leaned back against the couch. "It didn't feel brave. It felt like breathing."

Charity looked at her. "That's what truth does. When you speak it, it sets the air right again."

Ava reached for the letter, still folded on the table between them. "Do you think she knew we'd find it?"

"Yes."

"She hid it in the one place we'd return to."

Charity smiled. "And she made sure it would wait for us."

They sat in silence for a long time.

Outside the window, the city sparkled. But inside, all was still.

Ava finally spoke. "There's something else I want to do."

Charity looked over. "Tell me."

"I want to help the other girls find their mothers. Their sisters. Their names."

Charity nodded. "Then we'll build that bridge."

The next morning, headlines filled the newsfeeds.

"The Letter That Broke the Room."
"Ava Woods Reclaims Her Name."
"Two Sisters, One Legacy."

Journalists quoted the letter in full. Survivor networks began sharing it across platforms. Advocacy centers reached out to The Crossing requesting guidance, collaboration, funding for name restoration and case reconciliation. The movement had taken root.

And at the center of it all stood a woman who once had no name at all.

Ava Woods.

The wind that never surrendered.

Act 2 – Chapter 24

Title: "The Ones Left Behind"

The Crossing's headquarters buzzed with a kind of quiet electricity.

Charity stood in the conference room before a glass board now filled with colored sticky notes, maps, and linked names. At the center, written in blue marker, was the new initiative's title: **"Names Reclaimed."** It was not just a project; it was a declaration. One that would span cities and states, targeting foster care archives, sealed juvenile case files, and correctional facility rosters tied to the systemic erasure of child identities.

Ava entered with a stack of folders in her arms.

"These came from Philadelphia," she said, setting them on the table. "One of the shelters we contacted found seventeen case files flagged for 'alias reassignment.' Four of the children had siblings placed in other states."

Charity leafed through the files. "And no one ever reunited them."

Ava sat. "Because no one was supposed to."

They worked in silence for a moment, reading through names, tracing lines of connection that had been deliberately severed.

"This is going to take years," Ava finally said.

Charity looked at her. "Then we'll take years."

Across the table, Malcolm joined them, laptop open.

"I just got off the phone with Nora," he said. "She's arranged a closed-door summit with national foster care administrators, federal child welfare officials, and a handful of state representatives. They want to hear the plan."

Charity raised an eyebrow. "Or contain it."

"Both," Malcolm replied. "But you'll be there."

"Not just me," Charity said. "Us."

Ava looked at her.

"We started this together," Charity said. "We finish it together."

Three weeks later, they stood at the Capitol in a marble room flooded with natural light. Rows of padded chairs had been arranged in a semi-circle, microphones adjusted, bottled water placed carefully on each table. Attendees wore sharp suits and carefully neutral expressions.

Charity stepped to the center and introduced herself.

She did not begin with facts. She began with a name.

"Ava Woods," she said. "My sister. My proof."

She told the room the story they had already read in headlines but now heard in person. The fire. The erasure. The return. She did not spare the details, but she did not indulge them either. She made the room feel the cost of forgetting.

Ava stood and presented the proposal.

"We are asking for access," she said. "To records. To archives. To lists of children whose names were changed without cause or accountability. We are not here to punish. We are here to reconnect."

The room was still.

Then a voice from the back spoke.

"I appreciate your passion. But the system is more complicated than you're suggesting."

The speaker stood. A woman in her late fifties, tailored gray suit, government badge clipped to her belt. Her nameplate read: **Dr. Althea Randall, Director of National Child Services Reform Committee.**

"I've reviewed your proposal," she said. "And while it's well-intentioned, it assumes the system can absorb the emotional chaos of reopening hundreds of closed cases. Many of these records were sealed for a reason."

Charity met her gaze. "Some were sealed to protect children. Others were sealed to protect corruption."

Randall tilted her head slightly. "And how will you distinguish between the two?"

Ava stepped forward. "By asking the children."

Murmurs moved through the room.

Randall replied coolly, "Children forget. They misremember. Especially when trauma is involved."

Charity's voice remained even. "So did the adults. That's why we're still digging up the truth thirty years later."

Another official leaned forward. "And who exactly will oversee this effort? Who decides which names are pursued?"

Charity said, "The survivors. The families. The ones who lost someone."

Randall stepped closer, voice firm.

"You are proposing that we open a system already overburdened, underfunded, and politically fragile, all to chase paper trails that may or may not lead anywhere."

Charity replied, "They already led here."

A long pause followed.

Then the judge seated at the end of the panel cleared her throat.

"I've read the testimonies. I've seen the ledgers. And I believe the question isn't whether we can afford to do this. The question is whether we can afford not to."

After the hearing, Charity sat on the Capitol steps with Ava, her heels beside her on the marble, her breath slower than usual.

"She's going to push back," Ava said. "Dr. Randall. She's not done."

"I know."

"She doesn't want the records touched."

"Because she knows what's in them."

Ava leaned her head against her sister's shoulder. "Do you think we'll find more like us?"

Charity looked up at the sky, clouds drifting without hurry.

"I think we already have."

Back in New York, The Crossing's inbox filled with messages.

Hundreds of them.

Former foster children.

Social workers.

Adult adoptees who had always wondered why their names did not match their birth records.

And parents; aching, searching, still hoping.

Charity stood in the office with the printed pages spread across the table.

"They came," she whispered.

Ava nodded. "Because someone finally said their names."

Two days later, an encrypted message arrived at Charity's private email address. It was unsigned. There was no subject line. Just a scanned document.

She opened it slowly.

It was a list of case numbers, stamped with the seal of the **National Juvenile Placement Review Board.** Most had been redacted. But one name was circled.

Jasmine Reed.

Charity sat down hard.

Ava entered the room. "What is it?"

Charity turned the screen.

"She was in my first case file," she said. "One of the girls we tried to help when I started the foundation. She disappeared before we could place her."

Ava leaned closer. "You think she's still alive?"

"I think someone wants us to find her."

Malcolm walked in at that moment, phone in hand.

"We just got a call from someone inside Randall's office," he said. "There's a move to formally block your access request."

Charity stood. "Then we don't wait for permission."

Act 2 – Chapter 25

Title: "Still in Operation"

The document had only one name that mattered, and it was written in faded ink.

Jasmine Reed.

Charity stared at it for the hundredth time, her fingers tracing the circle someone had drawn around the name. She did not know who had sent it. The email had arrived in her secure inbox in the middle of the night, no subject, no signature, just a PDF scan of a decommissioned facility's transfer list.

But the timing was too precise to be coincidence. The summit. The testimony. The national attention. And now this.

Ava stepped into the room, her phone in hand.

"I pulled her intake record," she said. "She was marked as a non-communicative minor, assigned to Evergreen Renewal Academy. But here's the problem. Evergreen doesn't exist anymore."

Charity looked up. "When was it shut down?"

"It wasn't," Ava replied. "It was renamed. Twice."

Charity stood. "What's it called now?"

Ava handed her the phone.

"Thornhill Center for Behavioral Stability"

The name was sanitized, harmless on the surface. The website showed stock images of sunlight through windows and children coloring with staff. The language was all about "transition" and "guided development."

But Charity had seen this before.

The more innocent the name, the darker the truth.

Malcolm walked in carrying two large folders. "Nora just sent the full background on Thornhill. It was established three years after New Dawn closed, using leftover funding from a subsidiary of the same state contractor. It's in South Carolina, twenty miles outside Charleston."

Charity opened the folder and scanned the first few pages. "And Jasmine?"

"There's no formal record of her release," Malcolm said. "Her file ends in 2016."

Ava whispered, "That's nine years unaccounted for."

Charity looked up. "Then we go there."

The drive to Charleston was long, humid, and unnervingly quiet.

As they passed the state line, Charity glanced at Ava, who sat with her notebook open, listing every name that had come through The Crossing's inbox since the summit. She had highlighted those that mentioned missing siblings, changed names, or behavioral placements without cause.

There were now forty-six.

"How many do you think are still alive?" Ava asked.

Charity kept her eyes on the road. "Enough for this to matter."

When they reached Thornhill, it was mid-afternoon.

The facility sat just beyond a line of dense trees, the front gate framed by tall hedges and a discreet sign etched in bronze. A long gravel path led up to a circular driveway, where a receptionist stood behind tinted glass, wearing a badge and headset.

Charity parked in the visitor lot and stepped out slowly.

They had used The Crossing's credentials to request a tour two days earlier. No mention of Jasmine. No mention of New Dawn. Just an interest in potential "referral partnerships" for youth support services.

The receptionist buzzed them in with a practiced smile. "Welcome to Thornhill. You're on the list."

A tall man in a charcoal suit greeted them in the lobby.

"Ms. Woods, Ms. Fields. My name is Paul Danner, Director of Admissions. So pleased to welcome representatives from The Crossing. We've heard good things."

Charity shook his hand. "Thank you for having us."

"We always welcome collaboration," he said, gesturing for them to follow. "Our campus includes five cottages, an academic center, a behavioral wing, and recreational grounds. We serve both long-term and transitional youth populations."

Ava walked beside him. "How many students do you currently serve?"

"Just over eighty."

"And do you keep alumni files?" Charity asked.

Danner hesitated. "We maintain digital records for seven years, per state guidelines."

"And beyond that?"

"They're archived. Or destroyed. Depending on compliance."

Charity nodded.

She knew what that meant.

Destroyed meant hidden.

They walked through the grounds slowly, past quiet classrooms and manicured lawns. The place was too polished, too quiet. Charity watched the body language of the staff. Too quick to smile. Too ready with answers. She had learned to see past performance.

In one of the dorm wings, she spotted a corkboard labeled **"House Guidelines."** It listed mealtimes, chores, and an item labeled **Reflection Silence: 9 p.m. to 7 a.m.** Underneath, a typed rule: *No verbal communication permitted during this time, including whispering.*

Ava leaned toward her. "That's not therapeutic. That's control."

Charity whispered, "And it's exactly what they used at New Dawn."

They finished the tour in a small administrative conference room. Danner handed them a folder with a "Welcome Packet" and a QR code for a virtual brochure.

"If you'd like to schedule a second visit or speak with our clinical team, we're happy to coordinate," he said.

Charity smiled. "Actually, I'd like to request a specific alumni file. Jasmine Reed. Entered care in 2015."

The man's face remained unchanged, but his eyes faltered.

"I'm sorry," he said. "That name is not in our system."

Ava spoke gently. "Would it appear under another name?"

He looked between them, now wary.

"Our records are confidential."

Charity opened her purse and placed a single document on the table.

It was Jasmine's intake file, pulled from the National Juvenile Placement Review Board, with Thornhill's former name: Evergreen, clearly stamped in the top corner.

Danner stared at it.

"We're not here to damage your institution," Charity said. "We're here to find a person who may still be under your care."

Danner said nothing for a long moment.

Then he stood. "I need to make a call."

He left the room.

Charity turned to Ava. "We've got him."

Ten minutes later, the door reopened. But it was not Danner who entered.

A woman in a beige suit stepped inside, closed the door, and locked it.

"Ms. Woods. Ms. Fields," she said calmly. "I'm Dr. Elaine Mercer, legal counsel for Thornhill."

Charity stood. "Where is Jasmine?"

Dr. Mercer sat down across from them and folded her hands.

"I'm going to be direct. You're not going to find her here."

Ava asked, "Why not?"

"Because she was transferred three months ago to an adult residential facility. Her record is sealed. That's all I can tell you."

Charity's voice was quiet. "Did she ask for help?"

Mercer said nothing.

"Did she ever mention The Crossing? Did she write letters that were never sent?"

Mercer's gaze sharpened. "I'm advising you to leave this facility. Any further attempts to obtain sealed files may be construed as interference."

Charity stood. "We've been told that before."

Ava rose beside her. "But we're still here."

They walked out without another word.

Outside, the air was thick and hot.

Charity turned to Ava. "They're hiding her."

Ava nodded. "Then we'll uncover her."

Act 2 – Chapter 26

Title: "The Last Witness"

The rain came softly at first, a whisper on the windshield as the car eased through the outskirts of Beaufort, South Carolina. Charity gripped the steering wheel tighter, the wipers tracing slow arcs across the glass. In the passenger seat, Ava sat reviewing the intake files once more, her finger underlining Jasmine Reed's name.

According to the sparse notes from Thornhill's counsel, Jasmine had been transferred to a residential facility listed simply as **"St. Elm's Center for Adult Therapeutic Recovery."** No address was given. No contact number. Just a vague reference to Region 9 jurisdiction.

Charity had traced Region 9 to a cluster of counties along the coastal line. A buried page on an outdated state website had listed **St. Elm's** as a **closed-campus therapeutic stabilization program for vulnerable adults.**

"Closed campus," Ava muttered. "What does that even mean in plain English?"

Charity replied, "It means she can't leave."

They pulled into town near dusk. Beaufort was charming on the surface, cobblestone streets, white porches, river oaks draped with Spanish moss. But the silence was too clean, like a coat of paint hiding decay.

They checked into a local inn under assumed names and settled in quickly. The next morning, they visited a small records office attached to the county's health department.

The woman behind the desk wore a blue cardigan and half-moon glasses, her tone pleasant but cautious.

"I'm sorry," she said, typing slowly. "St. Elm's doesn't have a public-facing office anymore. Most of their records were consolidated during the last regional merger."

Charity leaned in. "Was Jasmine Reed among the transferred residents?"

The woman raised an eyebrow. "Are you family?"

"Yes," Ava said without pause. "She's, our cousin."

The clerk hesitated, then pulled a yellowing binder from under the counter.

"This isn't official, but..." She opened it and flipped through handwritten intake notes.

Ava leaned forward, scanning the list.

There it was.

Reed, Jasmine – Admitted 2016, Transferred from Evergreen/Thornhill – Status: Restricted.

Charity's voice was calm. "What does 'restricted' mean?"

The woman's face stiffened. "It means she was placed under long-term care with behavioral stabilization protocols. Visitors only by court order."

"Where is the facility located?" Ava asked.

The woman glanced at the office door, then back at them.

"Six miles out. Behind the state agricultural depot. But you didn't hear that from me."

Charity smiled softly. "Understood."

They followed a narrow road past cornfields and decaying barns until a steel gate came into view. A small security box stood on one side with no speaker, just a sign: *"Authorized Personnel Only. Deliveries Call Ahead."*

Malcolm, who had arrived that morning to join them, stood beside the passenger window and took a long look.

"This place wasn't meant to be found."

"No," Charity agreed. "But we found it anyway."

They parked off the road and approached on foot, circling the perimeter through the woods. After twenty minutes, they reached the backside of the property, where a small service entrance was partially hidden behind dense brush. A single camera pointed outward; its lens fogged with weather.

Charity reached for the gate.

Ava touched her shoulder. "Are we doing this?"

"We're not leaving without her."

Inside, the building was eerily quiet. The hallways smelled of bleach and something more sterile emptiness. Rooms lined the corridor, each door with a single viewing window. Some were open. Some were not.

They moved quickly, quietly.

Then Ava stopped.

"There," she whispered.

A door ahead had a tag.

Room 204 – Reed, J.

Charity stepped forward and knocked once.

No answer.

She opened the door slowly.

The room was dim but clean. A small bed, a wooden chair, and a woman seated beside the window, her posture stiff, her eyes staring out at nothing.

"Jasmine?" Charity asked softly.

The woman turned slowly.

Her face was older, drawn, eyes dull but alive. She blinked twice, as if trying to separate the moment from a dream.

Ava stepped beside her. "Jasmine, it's us. We're here to take you out."

Jasmine tilted her head. "No one comes here."

"We did," Charity said. "We're from The Crossing."

Jasmine's lips parted. "You're the one from the news."

Charity nodded. "Yes. I found my sister. Now we want to find the rest."

Jasmine's voice cracked. "They told me I was confused."

Ava knelt beside her. "You're not. You remember what they don't want you to."

Jasmine reached slowly under her mattress.

She pulled out a small, battered notebook, the edges frayed, the spine cracked.

"They didn't know I could write at night."

Charity opened the notebook gently.

Inside were pages of names. Dozens of them. First names. Nicknames. Sketches of faces. Clues.

"They called it Evergreen," Jasmine whispered. "But it wasn't green. It was quiet and locked. Some kids disappeared. They said it was behavior transfers."

Charity flipped to the last page.

A name was written in bold.

L. R. Carlisle – Program Director.

She whispered the name aloud.

Ava's face went pale.

"That's the man who signed my file at New Dawn."

Malcolm stepped inside. "He's not listed on any current rosters."

Charity looked at Jasmine. "Where is he now?"

Jasmine answered slowly. "He comes on Thursdays."

Charity glanced at her watch.

"It's Thursday."

Act 2 – Chapter 27

Title: "The Link They Never Expected"

The hallway outside Jasmine's room felt tighter with every breath. Charity stood frozen, notebook clutched against her chest, Ava beside her like a shadow made flesh. They had come to find a girl. Instead, they had unearthed a man, a name that connected New Dawn, Evergreen, Thornhill, and now, a federal network of silence.

L. R. Carlisle.

Charity remembered it now, barely visible on the bottom of a transfer form. Her father had circled it once in red ink in his notes, back when he had still believed he could bring everything into the light by naming it.

Ava spoke first.

"If he's coming today, we wait."

Malcolm stepped out from the shadow of the hallway, checking his watch. "If his pattern holds, he'll arrive at the staff entrance within the hour."

Charity closed Jasmine's notebook slowly and turned to Ava.

"Are you strong enough to see him?"

Ava's voice was clear. "I have been strong longer than I've been safe. Let's finish this."

They waited in the woods behind the service entrance, hidden among the tall grass and pines, the air thick with the buzz of insects and the scent of pine sap.

An hour passed.

Then, the gravel crunched.

A black sedan turned into the drive, slow and deliberate.

A man stepped out.

Tall. Slender. Silver-gray hair, pressed suit, clipboard in hand.

L. R. Carlisle.

He moved without rush, keys in hand, whistling softly under his breath.

Charity felt the breath catch in her throat.

"That's him," Ava whispered.

Carlisle disappeared into the building.

Charity turned to Malcolm. "Go to the front desk. Tell them we have a private meeting scheduled. Keep them distracted."

Malcolm nodded and left without a word.

Ava and Charity circled back to the side door, which Jasmine had quietly left unlocked for them.

Inside, they moved quickly and quietly. They knew the layout now. And they knew where Carlisle would go, Room 204.

When they reached the hall, they found him seated inside Jasmine's room, speaking to her in a low, patronizing voice.

"You don't need to think about those things," he said. "That world doesn't exist anymore."

Jasmine sat on the edge of the bed, silent.

Charity stepped through the doorway.

"She remembers just fine."

Carlisle turned, startled, but did not stand.

"You're not supposed to be here."

Charity entered fully, Ava right behind her.

"You're right. We're supposed to be gone."

Carlisle rose slowly, face tightening.

"You're trespassing. This is a secured facility."

Charity held up Jasmine's notebook.

"Your name is all over the history of these programs. You signed her intake form at Evergreen. You authorized behavior protocols at Thornhill. And before that, you were at New Dawn."

Carlisle did not respond.

Ava stepped closer.

"You changed my name."

He turned his eyes to her. For a flicker of a moment, something passed through them, not regret, but recognition.

"I was doing my job," he said.

"No," Charity said. "You were dismantling identities."

Carlisle's voice grew colder. "You have no idea how much we protected you from."

"From what?" Ava asked. "From truth? From family? From freedom?"

Carlisle turned toward the window, his hand trembling slightly on the sill.

"I did what I was told," he said.

"By whom?" Charity asked.

A long silence followed.

Then he said the name.

"Dr. Althea Randall."

Ava blinked. "The federal official trying to shut us down?"

Carlisle nodded.

"She was my supervisor at the State Office of Youth Rehabilitation. She drafted the first protocols for name reassignment. She believed identity was fluid, that it could be shaped by structure. And she believed that silence healed trauma."

"She believed in erasing children," Ava said.

"She believed in control," Carlisle corrected. "And she trained us all to follow."

Charity stepped closer. "So, you followed."

He looked at her. "She made sure I had no choice."

Charity held up the recorder from her coat pocket.

"You just made one."

Carlisle's face paled.

"Everything you've said is now on record."

He opened his mouth, then closed it again.

Ava took Jasmine's hand. "We're leaving. And she's coming with us."

Carlisle did not try to stop them.

He simply sank into the chair.

Charity turned at the doorway.

"You should prepare for what's coming."

He nodded once. "It's long overdue."

Back at The Crossing, the fallout was immediate.

Nora released the audio transcript within twelve hours. Headlines swelled with new urgency.

"Whistleblower Implicates Federal Director in Systemic Child Identity Suppression."

"'She Trained Us All': L. R. Carlisle Speaks."

By noon the next day, Dr. Randall's name was trending across every major platform.

The Department of Health and Human Services issued a statement acknowledging an internal investigation.

The Office of the Inspector General called for a hearing.

And The Crossing's servers flooded with thousands more names.

In her office, Charity stood by the window holding a printed copy of the transcript.

Her father's old desk sat behind her now, shipped from storage and restored, a symbol of what had endured.

Ava entered, carrying Jasmine's updated intake file.

"She's resting," Ava said. "But she wants to speak when she's ready."

Charity turned. "We'll let her choose."

Ava sat across from her.

"We were never supposed to find each other," she said. "We were never supposed to find any of this."

Charity smiled. "And yet, here we are."

Ava looked at the stack of new names.

"What do we do with all of them?"

"We do what Mama said," Charity replied. "We remember."

Act 2 – Chapter 28

Title: "A Letter with No Return Address"

The Federal Oversight Committee chambers had been prepared with exacting detail: microphones calibrated, notepads stacked, the seal of the United States gleaming behind the raised dais. Rows of reporters, policy analysts, and child advocacy leaders filled the public gallery. Cameras remained pointed but silent, red dots blinking patiently. Everyone in the room knew that history had arrived.

Charity sat in the first row, Ava beside her, Jasmine on her other side. Each woman wore a muted color, not because they wished to disappear, but because they had learned that presence need not shout to command attention.

When Dr. Althea Randall entered, the room stiffened. She wore a navy-blue suit, every button fastened, her chin raised as though she intended to conduct rather than answer. But her name placard did not sit behind the microphone. It faced the panel.

Today, she was not in command. Today, she was the witness.

Judge Willa Norcross began the proceedings with a formal tone.

"Dr. Randall, you are here in response to multiple whistleblower statements, a verified audio transcript, and official inquiries regarding your leadership and policies during your tenure with both state and federal child services agencies. This is not a criminal trial. But your words today will carry weight in the investigations that follow."

Randall adjusted the microphone. "Understood."

Charity leaned forward slightly, watching the woman who had nearly buried her sister with paper trails and policy language. Ava sat still, eyes never leaving Randall's face.

The first question came from a senator seated at the far left of the panel.

"Dr. Randall, did you authorize the use of name reassignment protocols for minors in long-term therapeutic custody?"

"Yes," Randall replied without hesitation. "At the time, we believed it provided a cognitive reset for children experiencing dissociation or extreme trauma. The goal was rehabilitation through identity stabilization."

The room shifted, barely perceptible.

"And did you, at any point, suppress records to prevent children from reconnecting with biological family members?"

Randall paused. "Records were sealed in compliance with then-active privacy mandates."

"But those seals were applied selectively. Some children's files were destroyed without court order. That is not a mandate. That is obstruction."

Randall folded her hands. "We made decisions based on what we believed was best for the child."

Ava whispered, "She's still hiding behind policy."

The lead investigator cleared his throat.

"Dr. Randall, did you have direct involvement with, or knowledge of the facility known as New Dawn Therapeutic Academy?"

Randall hesitated for the first time.

"Yes. I was consulted during its restructuring."

"And were you aware of the intake of Ava Woods, under the alias Aria Westfield?"

Randall's voice thinned. "I was informed she had no surviving family. Her reassignment was deemed appropriate under standard trauma masking protocols."

Charity stood.

The room turned.

"She did have family," Charity said, her voice calm but resolute. "Me."

Norcross gave a single nod. "Ms. Woods, you may approach."

Charity walked to the small podium at the side of the room.

"I was seven years old when my sister was taken from me. I was told she died. I was told our house fire was an accident. I was told my father's files were irrelevant. And I was told, repeatedly, that my questions would only hurt people."

She turned to Dr. Randall.

"You didn't just reassign names. You reassigned truth. You taught people to forget. But you failed to erase memory. You failed to bury justice. And you failed to silence us."

Dr. Randall said nothing.

Because there was nothing left to say.

That evening, back in New York, the sky stretched wide and silver. A storm lingered on the horizon, but the wind was still.

Charity returned to The Crossing, exhausted but upright. Her staff greeted her quietly. Nora left a handwritten note: *"You moved the earth today. Rest."*

She entered her office and found a package on her desk.

It was wrapped in brown paper, no return address, postmarked from Asheville.

Inside: a small wooden box.

She opened it slowly.

At the top was a letter.

Handwritten.

To my daughter, Charity,
If this reaches you, then you have uncovered what I could not finish. And I am proud of you in a way that no lifetime could fully hold.

Charity froze.

The handwriting was his.

There is something I never told you, and I regret that silence. The night I filed the judicial review, I knew they were coming. Not just for me, but for you and Ava. I arranged for a man I trusted to watch the house, someone who had once been a child in the very system I was trying to expose. He owed me nothing. He risked everything.

He carried you from the fire. You survived because people refused to forget you. Now, you are doing the same for others. That is what it means to bear the weight of light.

With love that never burns out,
Daddy

Her knees gave, but she did not fall. She sat on the floor of her office, letter pressed to her chest.

Ava found her there minutes later and sank to the carpet beside her.

Charity handed her the letter.

"He knew everything," she whispered. "And he still chose to stay."

Ava read it through trembling fingers, then placed it beside the box and leaned into her sister.

"What do we do now?" she asked.

Charity looked out at the approaching sky.

"We find the man who saved me."

Act 2 – Chapter 29

Title: "The Man Who Remembered"

The rain followed them from New York to Asheville, slow and steady, like a memory unspooling. Charity stared out the window of the rental car as droplets curved across the glass in long, deliberate trails. Ava sat beside her, silent, the letter from their father folded neatly in her lap.

Neither had spoken much since they left.

Some moments did not need words.

They arrived just before dusk, pulling up to the edge of a small mountain town tucked between green ridges and winding roads. The address that accompanied the letter's postmark had led them here, to a cabin at the end of a gravel road, partially hidden by cedar trees and covered in ivy, as if nature itself had chosen to protect it.

Malcolm followed in the second vehicle, pulling in behind them. He stepped out and surveyed the cabin with a cautious eye.

"Are we sure this is it?" he asked.

Charity nodded. "It has to be."

They approached slowly. A soft light glowed from inside the window. There was no mailbox, no doorbell, only a narrow plank porch with two wooden chairs and a boot scraper that had seen better years.

Charity raised her hand and knocked twice.

They waited.

Footsteps, then silence.

The door opened partway.

A man stood there. Older now, face worn by years, beard trimmed close, dark eyes steady behind wire-rimmed glasses. There was a faint scar just beneath his left eye.

He did not speak.

Charity stepped forward. "You carried me from the fire."

The man exhaled softly. "You remember."

"I remember now."

He opened the door fully.

"Come in."

The inside of the cabin was sparse but warm. A cast iron stove flickered softly in the corner. Shelves lined the back wall, filled with notebooks, old cassette tapes, and faded manila envelopes. The floor creaked with each step.

"My name is Ezra Merritt," the man said as he sat down. "I used to be one of them. The ones inside the system. But I couldn't stay that way."

Ava looked at him. "You worked for the state?"

Ezra nodded. "I was a records technician. My job was to log transfers, seal documents, and flag anything deemed 'unstable.' But I saw what they were doing. I saw how children disappeared into renamed buildings and came out... not at all."

Charity sat across from him. "You knew my father."

"I owed him my life," Ezra said. "He helped me clear my own juvenile record when I was sixteen. Believed I deserved more than a cell and a case number. Years later, when I saw what was happening with New Dawn, I reached out to him. He was already deep into the investigation."

"You warned him," Charity said.

"I tried. I told him they were moving quickly. That his review was making people nervous. He said he wouldn't stop."

Ava leaned forward. "Why did you stay?"

Ezra's face darkened. "To collect names. Evidence. I knew I couldn't stop the fire. But I could make sure it didn't kill everything."

Charity whispered, "You saved me."

"I found you in the hallway," Ezra said. "Your arm was burned, your mouth was covered in soot, but your eyes... your eyes were still fighting. I carried you out the back. Hid you behind the tool shed. They thought everyone was inside."

Ava's voice was soft. "They said I was alone."

Ezra looked at her. "You were never alone."

He rose slowly and crossed the room, pulling a box from a locked drawer in the corner. He set it on the table and opened it.

Inside were photographs, letters, fragments of files once believed destroyed.

"These are the names they tried to erase. Some of them I saved on microfilm, others I rewrote by hand. Your father gave me a list before he died. I've added to it over the years."

Charity picked up one of the pages.

At the top it read: **"Operation Sundown: Unauthorized Identity Reassignment, 1989–2002."**

She whispered the phrase. "Operation Sundown."

Ezra nodded. "That's what they called it behind closed doors. A transition strategy. Reduce state caseloads by moving high-need children into contracted facilities under new identities. The public was told they'd been placed in better care. In truth, they were being erased."

Malcolm flipped through another folder. "Why didn't you come forward?"

Ezra looked at him. "I was a ghost. They made sure of it. When I disappeared, I did so for a reason. If they knew I was alive, they'd find me. They'd erase me too."

Ava placed a hand on Ezra's.

"But you're here now."

Ezra met her gaze. "Because you found your way back."

He looked at Charity. "You both did."

They spent hours scanning the documents, cataloguing names, cross-referencing them with The Crossing's ledger. Some matched. Others filled in missing spaces. But one document stopped Charity cold.

It was a transfer memo with two names at the bottom.

Carlisle, L. R.
Randall, A.

Beside them, a third signature appeared.

Merritt, E.

Ezra looked down. "That was the last form I ever signed. I had no idea what they were doing until after. I spent the next ten years trying to undo it."

Charity touched the edge of the paper.

"This completes the chain," she said. "This proves Randall and Carlisle were not acting independently. It was a coordinated directive."

"And this," Ava said, holding up a folded paper from the box, "is the final case report filed on me."

She read it aloud.

Subject shows persistent attachment to imaginary sibling. Full reassignment recommended. Emotional severance necessary. Recommend controlled socialization and silencing periods.

Ava blinked slowly. "They called you imaginary."

Charity's voice was a whisper. "Then I guess I became their worst nightmare."

Before they left, Ezra handed them a second box.

"What's this?" Charity asked.

"The names that were never filed," Ezra replied. "Children I saw moved through the system but never saw again. They never made it into official logs. I wrote them down anyway."

Ava held the box like something sacred.

"You kept their names," she said.

Ezra nodded. "That's all some of them ever had."

Charity leaned forward and embraced him. She felt his arms shake as they wrapped around her.

"You gave me back everything," she whispered.

Ezra said nothing.

He just held on.

Act 2 – Chapter 30

Title: "The Archive Lives"

The press conference was scheduled for noon.

By 11:00 a.m., the steps outside The Crossing's New York headquarters were already filling with journalists, survivors, and onlookers. Microphones stood at attention on a single podium, with only one sign behind it:

"THE ARCHIVE PROJECT: WE REMEMBER."

Inside, the halls buzzed with urgency and reverence. Staff moved quickly but quietly, finalizing packets, adjusting the livestream setup, and escorting invited guests to reserved seats along the front row.

Charity stood in her office overlooking the scene.

The file box from Ezra sat open on her desk, each name entered into a digital ledger, uploaded into an encrypted server backed by five independent nonprofit servers. Every record had been verified twice. Every name had been prepared for release.

No one would be erased again.

Ava entered, dressed in soft gray, a gold pin over her heart shaped like an open book.

"They're ready," she said.

Charity turned. "Are you?"

Ava smiled. "Yes. And you?"

Charity nodded. "We were born for this."

By 12:03 p.m., the world was watching.

Livestream feeds ran across multiple platforms. Major news stations carried the broadcast live. State and federal officials tuned in from closed chambers. Some tuned in to support. Others tuned in hoping the story would slip or break. It did not.

Charity stepped up to the podium.

The air stilled.

"My name is Charity Elaine Woods," she began, voice steady. "I am the founder of The Crossing. I am a daughter, a sister, and a survivor of one of the longest-running systems of identity suppression in this nation's child welfare history."

She let the silence hold.

"For decades, thousands of children were taken from their families, renamed, relocated, and told their memories were lies. Some were orphaned. Others were separated by force. All were labeled as cases to manage, not lives to protect."

She held up a slim folder.

"This is *The Archive Project*. It contains the names of over three hundred and seventy children whose identities were suppressed, reassigned, or erased between 1989 and 2008. These are not just names. These are people. Some are with us today. Some are still missing. Some have passed. But every one of them deserves to be known."

The crowd was still. Faces were wet with tears. Hands clasped one another tightly.

"Today, we release their names to the public. Today, we stop the hiding."

She stepped back.

Ava took her place.

"My name is Ava Woods," she said, her voice soft but certain. "I lived under a name that was not mine for most of my life. I was told my family had died. I was told my voice was dangerous. I was told I was no one."

She looked out at the sea of faces.

"But I am here. And I remember."

She lifted the locket their mother had hidden years ago and opened it, revealing the tiny photograph of them as girls.

"We dedicate this archive to the families who never stopped searching. To the children who found their way back. And to those still waiting."

Behind them, a large screen lit up with scrolling names.

One by one.

A hush fell again.

Jasmine Reed's name appeared first.

Then Devin Foster.

Then Aria Westfield, with a note: *Known as Ava Woods. Identity Recovered.*

Each name that followed added weight to the silence.

No music played.

There were no introductions, no applause.

Just memory.

Just truth.

That night, back inside The Crossing, Charity and Ava sat on the rooftop garden with Malcolm, Jasmine, and several of the recovered survivors. Small lanterns lined the terrace, each one lit in remembrance.

Jasmine leaned over the railing, looking out at the skyline.

"I didn't think the world would ever say our names out loud," she said.

"They said them today," Ava replied. "And they'll keep saying them."

Malcolm nodded toward Charity. "We've had calls from five state departments requesting archive access. Two congressional aides want meetings. A law firm is offering to provide pro bono support to every family ready to file civil claims."

Charity sipped her tea. "Then we get ready."

Jasmine looked at her. "What's next?"

Charity turned toward the group.

"Next, we finish what our father started. We take this to court."

Three days later, a sealed envelope arrived at The Crossing.

It bore the seal of the Department of Justice.

Charity opened it at her desk, surrounded by her legal team.

The top page read:

**IN RE: UNITED STATES VS. CARLISLE ET AL.
OPENING DATE OF FEDERAL TRIAL PROCEEDINGS CONFIRMED.
PLAINTIFFS: THE CROSSING, REPRESENTING ARCHIVE PROJECT FAMILIES.**

Ava entered just as she read the final line.

Charity looked up.

"It's happening," she said.

Ava took the envelope and read the words slowly.

For a long time, neither one of them spoke.

Then Charity whispered, "This will be a fight."

Ava placed a hand on her sister's.

"Then we fight with names. We fight with memory. And this time, we win."

Act 3 – Chapter 31

Title: "In the Eyes of the Court"

The courtroom was larger than Charity expected.

Not in size, but in silence. It held space like a cathedral, with high windows that allowed light to fall only where it chose. Rows of polished benches stretched back toward the gallery, already filling with media, survivor advocates, government observers, and families carrying photographs.

At the front, beneath the seal of the United States District Court, stood the bench, presided over by **Judge Elise Bradford**, a woman known for her poise and precision. Her gray hair was pulled into a low bun, her glasses perched with the casual exactness of someone who missed nothing.

Charity sat at the plaintiff's table beside Nora, who shuffled through binders, tabs, and legal pads with calm efficiency. Across the aisle, the defense team was assembling—seven attorneys in gray and navy suits, each reviewing files with studied cool.

Among them sat **Dr. Althea Randall**, stone-faced, hands folded in front of her.

Ava sat two rows behind Charity, her eyes fixed forward, her fingers holding the edge of her seat. Jasmine sat beside her, hands clasped, lips pressed tight. Malcolm stood near the rear with the press coordinator, overseeing real-time updates.

The judge called the court to order.

"All rise."

Everyone stood.

"This court is now in session for proceedings regarding *The United States v. Carlisle et al.*, inclusive of contributing agents and systemic negligence under Title IX, juvenile protections, and federal fraud statutes related to The Archive Project."

Charity inhaled slowly.

It was beginning.

Nora opened with the plaintiff's statement.

She spoke in simple, steady terms: children taken, names reassigned, identities buried beneath bureaucratic language and contract-funded secrecy. She cited precedents, federal reporting failures, and the cover-up spanning three decades. She spoke for twenty-three minutes.

Then she said the words everyone had been waiting for:

"The first witness we will call is Ms. Charity Elaine Woods."

A low murmur moved through the gallery.

Charity stood.

As she walked toward the stand, the courtroom shifted with her. Some leaned in. Others held their breath. She had been the face of the movement, but now she was not giving a speech. She was giving testimony.

She took the oath.

Sat down.

And looked directly at Judge Bradford.

Nora approached.

"Ms. Woods, what is your current role?"

"I am the founder and executive director of The Crossing, a national child advocacy organization focused on identity restoration and systemic trauma recovery."

"Why did you found The Crossing?"

Charity looked out across the courtroom.

"Because I lived through what it was built to fight."

Nora nodded. "Can you explain?"

Charity's voice did not waver.

"When I was seven, I survived a house fire. I was told it was an accident. My parents were killed. My sister was presumed dead. I later learned the fire was not an accident. It was a cover-up. My father, Judge Elijah Woods, was in the process of exposing a network of institutional abuse. My sister was taken, renamed, and hidden. I was placed with guardians and told to forget."

"And did you?"

"I tried," she said softly. "But memory is stubborn. Especially when it's tethered to truth."

The courtroom was silent.

Nora continued.

"In your investigation, did you find evidence of coordinated name reassignment?"

"Yes."

"Can you provide an example?"

Charity gestured toward Ava in the gallery.

"My sister. Her birth name was Ava Woods. She was renamed Aria Westfield. Then later, Ria Fields. All without her consent. Without any family notified."

"And did your father investigate these practices before his death?"

Charity held up a folder.

"Yes. This is his sealed testimony, recorded three weeks before he died. He named several officials involved in the operation. Including L. R. Carlisle and Dr. Althea Randall."

The defense immediately objected.

"Your Honor, we request a recess to review this material."

Judge Bradford shook her head. "Objection overruled. The testimony has been on record for twenty-one days and was included in discovery."

Nora nodded and continued.

"Ms. Woods, what is *The Archive Project*?"

"It's a digital and physical registry of children whose identities were changed through unauthorized or unethical means. We compiled it from recovered records, whistleblower documents, and firsthand testimony."

"And how many names are in the Archive?"

Charity answered, "Three hundred and seventy-six."

"Of those, how many have been confirmed?"

"Two hundred and eleven."

"And how many remain unaccounted for?"

Charity paused.

"One hundred and sixty-five."

Her voice softened.

"Some of them are likely deceased. Some are still in the system under new names. Some may never know who they were."

Nora stepped back.

"No further questions."

The defense approached.

The lead attorney, a tall man with a silver tie and clipped tone, addressed her directly.

"Ms. Woods, you are not a licensed attorney or investigator, correct?"

"Correct."

"You are not a trained forensic archivist or child psychologist."

"No."

"You are a marketing executive."

"I was," Charity replied. "Now I fight for children."

"Do you believe that emotional testimony should dictate federal reform?"

"I believe truth should," she said. "And sometimes, truth cries when it speaks."

He stiffened slightly, then pressed forward.

"Isn't it true that The Crossing has received over two million dollars in donations since the release of *The Archive Project*?"

"Yes," Charity said. "And all of it has been spent locating, housing, and representing survivors, survivors your clients tried to erase."

The courtroom stirred.

"No further questions," he muttered.

After her testimony, Charity stepped down and returned to her seat. Her hands were damp, her heartbeat loud in her ears. Ava squeezed her hand.

"You were perfect," she whispered.

Charity exhaled. "I told the truth."

That evening, back at the hotel, Ava received a message.

A quiet knock came at her door twenty minutes later.

Charity opened it.

Ava stood holding a letter.

"This was left for me."

They sat on the bed together as Ava unfolded the page.

It was brief.

Ava,
I have agreed to testify. But I will only do so if you ask me to. I promised your father I would protect you from the weight of all this. But I see now that you're stronger than we ever imagined.
If you ask me to come forward, I will.
Ezra

Ava placed the letter on her lap.

Charity looked at her. "What do you want to do?"

Ava stared at the wall.

Then answered.

"I want him to speak. Because I don't want to carry the silence anymore."

Act 3 – Chapter 32

Title: "A Name That Shook the Room"

The morning air was crisp as the courthouse filled again. Inside, the atmosphere was more charged than the day before. Word had spread that a new witness was coming forward, one not listed on the original docket. Survivors sat shoulder to shoulder in the gallery, some holding laminated copies of names from the Archive. Reporters clustered near the aisle, pens ready.

Charity sat near the front, her hands clasped, her eyes steady.

Ava sat beside her, calm on the outside, but her fingers trembled against the edge of her seat.

Malcolm entered quietly and nodded once. "He's here."

Nora stepped to the front and addressed the judge.

"Your Honor, the plaintiffs request to call a supplemental witness: Mr. Ezra Merritt."

A ripple moved through the gallery.

Judge Bradford glanced down at the docket, then back up. "Proceed."

Ezra entered from the witness room, wearing a plain dark coat, his frame upright though leaner than his years. He walked with quiet intent, pausing before the bailiff to take the oath.

"I do."

He sat, looking not at the attorneys, not at the judge, but at Charity and Ava.

Nora approached the stand.

"Mr. Merritt, could you state your occupation during the years 1989 through 1998?"

"I was a records technician for the State Office of Youth Rehabilitation. My job was to process intake reports, maintain transfer documents, and log behavioral evaluations for juveniles placed in long-term facilities."

"Were you involved in Operation Sundown?"

Ezra nodded. "Yes. At the time, I did not know the full scope. I signed forms. I filed names. I sealed records. I believed I was doing administrative work. I later learned I was helping erase people."

Gasps broke in the gallery.

Nora's voice remained composed.

"Do you recognize the defendant, Dr. Althea Randall?"

"Yes. She was my direct supervisor for four years."

"Did she direct you to change or destroy any documentation related to juvenile identity?"

"Yes. In 1992, I was given a list of twenty-two names. I was told to assign new identities, purge their existing files from state systems, and refile them under therapeutic aliases. These were not adopted children. These were wards of the state."

"Did you comply?"

"I did. At first."

Ezra took a breath, then turned slightly toward the judge.

"But one name caught me off guard. Ava Woods. I knew her father. He was a judge with a reputation for integrity. I flagged the reassignment. I was reprimanded. A week later, Judge Woods's home burned down."

Silence hit like a stone.

Ezra continued, voice tightening.

"I knew it wasn't coincidence. That night, I drove to Shady Grove. I watched the house. When the fire started, I ran inside. I found a girl in the hallway, barely conscious. I carried her out and hid her until responders arrived. Then I disappeared."

He looked toward Charity.

"She was the girl."

Judge Bradford spoke gently. "Mr. Merritt, did you preserve any evidence during your years in the system?"

Ezra opened a small folder and lifted a photograph.

"I preserved this."

He handed it to the bailiff.

It was a scanned memo, dated, signed by Randall, co-signed by Carlisle, and at the bottom, another name.

L. J. Gaines.

Nora asked, "Who is that?"

Ezra's voice darkened. "Dr. Gaines ran facility oversight under the alias L. J. He was the one who designed the reassignment evaluation form used at both New Dawn and Evergreen. But that's not the shock."

He pulled a second paper from his folder.

A birth certificate. Faded. Smudged. But legible.

Nora leaned in. Then froze.

She looked at the judge.

"Permission to display this document to the court?"

"Granted."

The screen behind the bench lit up.

The document appeared.

Name: Lawrence Jacob Gaines
Relation: Adoptive son of Henry Wells, Former Commissioner of Shady Grove County

The room gasped.

Charity stood.

"That's the man who ordered the fire."

Ava's voice trembled. "It was his son?"

Ezra nodded slowly. "Yes. L. R. Carlisle is a name. But his birth name was Lawrence Jacob Gaines."

Judge Bradford raised a hand.

"We are entering new territory. Does the defense wish to respond?"

One of the attorneys stood, clearly shaken.

"Your Honor, we were unaware of this connection. We request a recess to validate the documents."

"Request denied," Judge Bradford said. "The witness has presented evidence that connects multiple key individuals under the umbrella of familial and systemic collusion. The record will reflect this."

Outside, cameras swarmed.

Inside, Ezra stepped down, unsteady but held upright by purpose.

Charity met him in the hallway, arms wrapped around him before he could speak.

"You gave us everything," she whispered.

Ezra said nothing. But he smiled.

Ava approached, tears welling.

"They tried to turn you into a ghost," she said. "But you became the map."

Ezra placed a hand on her shoulder.

"Just promise me one thing."

"Anything."

"When this is over, keep remembering."

That evening, Nora held a press briefing on the courthouse steps.

She addressed the crowd clearly, firmly.

"We have confirmed that L. R. Carlisle, one of the principal architects of juvenile identity reassignment programs across four states, is the biological son of Commissioner Henry Wells, the man identified in the sealed recording of Judge Elijah Woods. This is no longer a question of negligence. This is legacy. And we are ready to confront it."

Charity and Ava stood behind her, holding hands.

The world now knew what they had always known.

Erasure was not policy. It was inheritance.

And the only cure was light.

Act 3 – Chapter 33

Title: "The Weight of the Invitation"

Three days after Ezra's testimony, the courthouse halls had changed.

There was no more polite disinterest. No more speculative glances. Every hallway buzzed with attention, and every face seemed aware that something irreversible had happened.

Judge Elise Bradford had called an emergency conference after reviewing the submitted documents linking Lawrence Jacob Gaines, formerly known as L. R. Carlisle, to Henry Wells. Following a series of sealed-door discussions with federal officials, she made her decision.

The gallery was full again. Journalists lined the edges. Survivors, legal aides, students, and civic leaders pressed in with quiet anticipation.

Judge Bradford sat higher than usual, her gavel resting gently beside her notes.

"This court," she began, "has heard the testimonies of survivors, former officials, whistleblowers, and archivists over the last twelve days. What has come to light is not merely a case of negligence or isolated corruption, but a sustained and coordinated operation designed to conceal children by erasing their identities, obstructing justice, and perpetuating silence through systemic manipulation."

No one moved.

"I am ordering a full federal inquiry into all state-contracted child welfare programs operated under the Office of Youth Rehabilitation from 1988 through 2008, including satellite facilities operating under subsidiary names. This inquiry will include New Dawn Therapeutic Academy, Evergreen Renewal Center, Thornhill, and any facilities cross-referenced in The Archive Project ledger."

Applause was forbidden in federal court.

But the tears were not.

Charity exhaled slowly. Ava reached over and held her hand.

The judge continued.

"I am also directing the United States Department of Health and Human Services, along with the Office of Civil Rights, to convene a new independent oversight committee for reform and reparation recommendations."

She paused, then looked directly at Ava.

"And, Ms. Woods, you are hereby extended an invitation to serve as one of the founding members of that committee."

Ava's mouth parted slightly.

Judge Bradford's voice softened.

"You have lived the very story this court is investigating. You have survived the consequence of systems meant to protect. And you have stood with grace, clarity, and strength. If you choose to accept this invitation, your voice will shape policy moving forward."

Ava's reply came slowly, quietly.

"Thank you, Your Honor. May I have time to consider it?"

"Of course," the judge replied. "You have earned every minute."

Outside the courthouse, the air felt different.

The reporters did not shout.

They waited.

And Ava did not speak.

Not yet.

Charity shielded her from the questions with a simple gesture and guided her into the waiting car. Once inside, the silence was full.

"You, okay?" Charity asked.

"I don't know," Ava said honestly.

She looked out the window, the courthouse disappearing behind them.

"I thought I wanted justice. And I do. But I don't know if I can be part of the system that failed us."

Charity nodded slowly. "Sometimes change has to come from within."

Ava shook her head. "And sometimes it needs to be built from scratch."

Back at The Crossing, they met with Nora and Malcolm in the boardroom.

The table was covered in folders and laptops, updates pouring in from advocacy networks across the country. New names were being submitted to The Archive every hour. Families were calling to ask for support in locating siblings. State offices had begun internal audits.

The wave had turned.

But Ava sat quietly, apart from the documents, lost in her thoughts.

Charity watched her.

Nora approached gently. "It's a lot."

Ava nodded. "I didn't expect the offer."

"You earned it," Nora said. "But that doesn't mean you owe it anything."

Ava turned. "How do you know when you're ready?"

Nora smiled gently. "You don't. You just walk anyway."

That night, Ava returned to the rooftop alone.

The city below sparkled like a promise, or a dare.

She sat beneath a string of garden lights and opened the locket her mother had left them. Inside, their childhood photo still smiled, unchanged. Ava held it close to her heart.

Then she opened her notebook.

She wrote slowly, deliberately:

**"Dear Mama,
They asked me to lead.
They asked me to build what never protected us.
I don't know what the answer is yet.
But I know this:
You didn't raise silence.
You raised truth."**

She closed the notebook and looked up at the stars.

Then she whispered, "Maybe it's time."

The next morning, she stood in front of the press with Charity by her side.

The statement was short.

"My name is Ava Woods. I accept the invitation to serve on the national oversight committee. I will not serve to protect a system. I will serve to protect children."

Charity stepped forward.

"And The Crossing will remain independent. We are not dissolving. We are expanding. This is not the end. This is the beginning of full restoration."

Reporters raised hands.

Questions poured forward.

But the sisters smiled.

Because they had already said everything they needed.

Act 3 – Chapter 34

Title: "The Invitation to Return"

The committee met for the first time inside a private conference chamber near Capitol Hill. The table was wide and round, by design: no head, no throne. The air hummed with tension and potential. Ava sat quietly at her designated seat, her name etched into a simple brass placard: *Ava Woods, Survivor Advocate.*

Across from her were department officials, mental health experts, and nonprofit leaders. Beside her sat a young man named Thomas Raines, formerly known as Isaac Monroe. He had been adopted under a false name at eight and had recently reconnected with his birth family through The Archive Project.

He spoke first.

"I think we start with what wasn't done. No one listened. Not to us. Not to the ones who knew."

Heads nodded around the table.

Ava added, "We don't need another statement of concern. We need actionable oversight. Every sealed record should be reviewed. Every child assigned a new identity should be tracked and offered their truth."

A woman across the table leaned in. "That could take years."

Ava didn't flinch. "Then let it."

She was no longer asking permission.

She was building the foundation.

Back in New York, Charity stood in her office, sorting through a thick packet marked **Confidential Proposal**.

It had arrived that morning by courier. The return label came from **North Carolina Department of Youth Services**.

Inside was a typed letter from the regional commissioner, a woman named Lydia Sampson. She had watched the hearings. She had reviewed the findings. And she had an offer.

Charity read the last paragraph twice.

"We would like to formally offer you the opportunity to lead the development of a new memorial and education center on the site of your former childhood home in Shady Grove, North Carolina. The facility will serve as a public reckoning and an archive of reform. If you choose to accept, you will design its vision. We will fund it. And we will listen."

Charity set the letter down and stared out the window.

The ache in her chest was not fear. It was memory pressing against her ribs.

She walked into the boardroom where Malcolm and Nora were reviewing The Crossing's next expansion plan.

"I need to go back," she said.

Malcolm looked up. "To Shady Grove?"

Charity nodded. "They want to build something. On the land where my life ended and started again."

Nora's eyes softened. "And they want you to define it?"

"Yes."

"Then you should go."

The plane landed just before sunset.

The air in Shady Grove was heavier than Charity remembered: warm, close, quiet. She stepped off the tarmac into the waiting car. The driver nodded to her politely and handed her a folder.

Inside was a map of the land her family once owned.

Lot 17.

Now overgrown and undeveloped, the space sat between two crumbling fence lines, wild grass curling around the base of the old foundation stones. The county had maintained ownership after the fire, keeping the land listed as dormant.

She arrived just after dusk.

The field was silent.

She stepped out of the car and walked to the edge of the property. In the distance, she could still make out the outline of where the porch once stood. The trees her mother had planted were taller now, gnarled at the base but still upright.

She knelt, placing her hand on the earth.

And she whispered, "I'm home."

The next day, she met with Lydia Sampson, a sharply dressed woman in her late forties with quiet fire behind her voice.

"I want to be clear," Lydia said, "This isn't about erasing what happened. It's about making sure it's never forgotten."

Charity nodded. "Then I'm interested."

Lydia opened her folder. "The site would be yours to shape. We envision it as a living memorial: part museum, part storytelling center, part advocacy hub. But it must start with your voice."

Charity paused. "I'd need control over the messaging."

"You'll have it."

"I'd need funding for survivor travel and education partnerships."

"Granted."

"And I want the front wall to bear names: not photos, not quotes. Names."

Lydia nodded. "Done."

Charity exhaled.

It was time.

That evening, Charity called Ava.

She stepped out onto the inn's porch, the sky overhead streaked with indigo and silver. Fireflies blinked at the edge of the field.

Ava answered on the second ring.

"You made it," she said.

"I'm looking at the house," Charity replied. "Or where it used to be."

A pause.

"Does it hurt?" Ava asked.

Charity looked down at the ground beneath her feet.

"Yes. But it doesn't crush me anymore."

"I'm proud of you," Ava said.

Charity smiled. "They want to build a memorial center. Right here. They want me to lead it."

"What do you want?"

"I want to turn this graveyard into a lighthouse."

"Then do it."

Later that night, she walked to the center of the field.

She stood where the fireplace used to be.

She closed her eyes.

And she saw them.

Her mother, reading on the couch. Her father, walking in from the rain. Ava, twirling in ballet shoes too big for her feet. Herself, humming softly, arms wrapped around a book.

Not lost.

Not erased.

Just waiting.

She opened her eyes.

And began to plan.

Act 3 – Chapter 35

Title: "A House Made of Names"

The land spoke in quiet ways. Wind moving through tall grass. Roots cracking beneath the surface. The earth itself had not forgotten what happened here. Neither had Charity.

She stood at the center of the field, sketchpad in hand, the old oak tree casting a long shadow behind her. On the page, she had drawn the beginnings of the memorial, simple lines, open space, and a single wall in the center. Not for photos. Not for curated plaques. Just names. Hundreds of them.

At the bottom of the sketch, she had written:

Let their names outlive the silence.

A local builder arrived around noon, a man named Gerald Benton. Gray-haired and sharp-eyed, he carried blueprints beneath his arm and reverence in his voice.

"Miss Woods," he said, shaking her hand. "I was a boy when the fire happened. We didn't know what we know now. But I'd be honored to help build what should've always been here."

Charity nodded. "Then let's start."

They walked the grounds together, mapping the boundaries. The front would hold the name wall. Behind it, a garden. Beyond that, a center for education, archiving, and reflection. The center would have no gates. No fences. Just a threshold, wide and welcoming.

"I want every child who walks through here to feel seen," Charity said.

Gerald made notes.

"I want the bricks in the courtyard to bear names too," she added. "Names of those still missing."

He looked at her, voice low. "You really think this will change anything?"

Charity smiled. "No. I think it will change everything."

Meanwhile, in Washington, Ava sat in a sharply lit hearing room, facing the full panel of the newly formed National Oversight Committee. Her position as survivor advocate had quickly become more than ceremonial. Her voice carried weight. And that weight now met resistance.

Across the table sat two senior agency consultants who had objected to her most recent proposal: mandatory review of all sealed juvenile records from 1990 to 2010.

"This review would be logistically overwhelming," said a woman with a clipped tone and a tightly woven bun. "Thousands of documents, most filed under now-defunct facilities."

Ava didn't flinch. "Overwhelming isn't the same as impossible."

Another consultant, older and visibly tired, leaned forward.

"Some of these cases were sealed with good reason, abuse protections, privacy laws, adoption confidentiality. Reopening them may retraumatize families."

Ava folded her hands.

"And what do you think being erased did?"

The room was still.

She continued.

"No child should wake up not knowing who they are because someone decided their name was inconvenient. I'm not asking for chaos. I'm asking for honesty."

The moderator, a balanced woman named Selena Morales, finally spoke.

"Let's give Ms. Woods space to formalize her recommendation. We'll place it on the next voting agenda."

Ava nodded, lips tight.

The meeting adjourned.

As she left, Thomas Raines caught up with her.

"You were good in there," he said. "Firm. Focused."

She shook her head. "They think I'm emotional."

"Let them," he said. "Emotion is what got us this far."

She smiled faintly. "Thanks, Thomas."

Back in Shady Grove, Charity stood beside the old tree as the first shipment of bricks arrived. Each was blank. Ready to carry a name. Volunteers began unloading them quietly.

She walked among them, clipboard in hand, assigning sections.

A woman approached her with a hesitant voice.

"My sister was in New Dawn," she said. "I... I never knew what happened to her. But her name's in your archive. Will her name be on the wall?"

Charity nodded. "Yes. If you'd like, you can place her name there yourself."

The woman's eyes filled. "She was only eleven."

Charity reached out and gently took her hand.

"Then this place belongs to her too."

That night, Charity called Ava.

"You sound tired," Ava said.

"I am," Charity replied. "But good tired."

They talked for a while, catching up on committee developments and site progress.

"I'm proud of you," Ava said.

"You always say that."

"Because I always mean it."

There was a pause.

Then Ava added, "They're pushing back hard."

Charity's tone grew quieter. "Do you feel safe there?"

"I feel necessary."

Charity smiled. "Then you're exactly where you should be."

They hung up a few minutes later, both quieter, both stronger.

The next morning, Charity met with the design team to finalize the layout of the indoor archive wing.

"I want a listening room," she said. "No visuals. Just voices. Survivor recordings. Unfiltered."

The lead architect, a young woman with ink on her hands and conviction in her voice, nodded.

"I know exactly how to build that."

They marked the center of the floor with tape.

"This is where it starts," Charity said.

One name.

One voice.

One space where silence no longer wins.

Meanwhile, Ava returned to the oversight committee chamber the next day with her proposal in hand.

She placed it on the table and stood.

"I am formally requesting a task force be created to unseal juvenile records and reunite families whose identities were altered without consent. I understand this will take years. I understand it will be painful. But so is forgetting."

The room waited.

Selena Morales nodded. "We will add your motion to the agenda."

Later that evening, Ava found a note slipped under her office door.

It was unsigned.

It read:

"Keep going. Some of us are rooting for you quietly."

She held it for a long moment, then folded it neatly and tucked it into her notebook.

She wasn't doing this alone.

Not anymore.

Act 3 – Chapter 36

Title: "What the Ground Would Not Keep Buried"

The groundbreaking ceremony for the Shady Grove memorial was quiet by design.

Charity didn't want fanfare. She wanted intention. A group of twenty stood scattered across the grassy field; survivors, local advocates, state officials, and builders who had watched the land sit still for far too long. A wooden sign marked the future entrance: **The Elijah and Leah Woods Center for Truth and Restoration.**

Ava had flown in the night before, standing at Charity's side in soft gray, her expression reverent but unreadable. Jasmine stood behind them, holding a small, engraved brick with her own name on it. One of hundreds that would form the path.

Charity stepped forward with a spade in hand.

"This ground is not cursed," she said, her voice clear. "It's sacred. Because what they tried to destroy here lived on. In memory. In truth. In us."

She pressed the spade into the earth.

The soil turned.

And the silence broke.

Later that evening, the two sisters sat beneath the old oak tree, now strung with lanterns. The workers had gone for the day. The sky was slow and darkening, warm with the color of deep summer.

"I still see it sometimes," Ava said. "The fire. The ceiling falling."

Charity nodded. "I see Mama's hand pushing me toward the door."

They sat in silence.

Then Ava turned. "Do you think we've done enough?"

Charity looked at her. "Enough for what?"

"For them to rest."

Charity's eyes softened. "I don't know. But I think they're proud."

Ava leaned her head on Charity's shoulder.

"I want to believe that."

The next morning, Charity arrived early to walk the site alone before the builders returned. The dew was still clinging to the grass, and the air smelled of soil and something older.

She moved toward the corner of the property, what used to be the back of the house, near where her father's study once stood.

There, tucked under the edge of a rotting floor beam they had just uncovered, something caught her eye.

Paper. Thick. Weathered. Folded neatly into a square.

She crouched and carefully removed it.

It was an envelope. Unsealed. Yellowed. No name on the front.

Inside, a single sheet of lined paper.

"They're watching me now. If this is ever found, know this, Carlisle isn't alone. He's not the top. There's someone else. Higher. Hidden. Look at the funding trails. It all begins with Crescent Holdings."

No signature. No date. But the handwriting.

Charity recognized it.

It was her father's.

Charity stood frozen, the wind still around her.

Crescent Holdings.

She had seen the name buried in one of the Thornhill subsidiary reports but hadn't questioned it. It had looked like one of the many shell companies used for asset transfers.

She ran back to the temporary operations tent and flipped open her laptop.

Within minutes, she had pulled the records again.

Crescent Holdings wasn't a contractor. It was a **private trust**, based in North Carolina, with silent investments across dozens of state contracts: mental health services, juvenile reform, foster placement support. The trust was founded in 1983 by three names.

Two were dead.

The third was very much alive.

David E. Marsh.

Former U.S. Senator.

Philanthropist.

Current chair of the **National Child Protection Reform Alliance**.

Charity stepped back from the screen.

This was no longer just about the past.

She called Ava.

"I found something."

"Is it real?" Ava asked.

"Yes. And dangerous."

That evening, a man appeared at the memorial site.

Charity had stayed late to walk the land once more. The sun had dipped low, and the light was long and golden when she heard footsteps behind her.

She turned.

A man stood there, tall, dressed in a plain brown blazer, clean-shaven, with a familiar gait.

He stopped just outside the taped boundary.

"You must be Charity," he said. "I knew your father."

Charity's eyes narrowed. "Who are you?"

"My name is Graham Lester. I worked under Senator Marsh for eight years. I've come to warn you."

"Warn me?"

He stepped forward slowly.

"There are lines you're about to cross. The names you've uncovered are not the end. They're the beginning. Crescent Holdings isn't just a trust. It's a gate."

Charity remained still.

"Then let it open."

Lester shook his head. "You don't understand. There were decisions made that cannot be reversed. If you push this too far, people will not just resist. They will retaliate."

Charity folded her arms. "Is that a threat?"

"It's a fact."

She studied him. "Why tell me this?"

"Because I saw your father go down fighting. And I couldn't save him. But I can give you one chance. Walk away from Crescent. Focus on what you've built. Let the past be the past."

Charity stepped closer, her voice low and firm.

"You're too late. We already remembered."

Lester held her gaze for a long moment.

Then he nodded once and turned to leave.

Charity called after him. "You said you knew my father."

He paused. "I did."

"Then you should know I don't scare easily."

He didn't turn around.

But he smiled.

That night, Charity and Ava sat on a video call with Nora and Malcolm.

"There's a deeper tier," Charity said. "Our father knew. And it's still operating."

Nora rubbed her temples. "If Crescent's involved at the federal level, we'll need whistleblower protection. Possibly a grand jury."

Malcolm added, "We'll need allies in the press. Quiet ones."

Ava nodded. "And I'll bring this to the committee. On record."

Charity looked down at the letter again.

"We're not finished."

Malcolm smiled faintly. "Not even close."

Act 3 – Chapter 37

Title: "The Vote Behind Closed Doors"

The marble hallway outside the Oversight Committee chamber was colder than usual. Ava stood alone, folder clutched in her arms, her heels silent against the polished floor. Inside that folder were five pages, a printed summary of Crescent Holdings' shell investments, a scanned memo from Judge Elijah Woods, and an organizational chart that revealed too much for comfort.

At the bottom of every funding trail was the same name: **David E. Marsh**.

Former senator. National figurehead. And now, the silent architect of a system designed to suppress the truth.

Ava took a slow breath and stepped into the chamber.

The room quieted the moment she entered. Her seat was waiting at the crescent-shaped table. Across from her, nine members of the committee shuffled papers, shifted in leather chairs, or simply stared.

Selena Morales, chairwoman of the committee, gave a small nod.

"You may proceed."

Ava stood. She didn't clear her throat. She didn't glance down at notes. She looked each member in the eye, one by one.

"Over the last several months, we have traced systemic child identity erasure across more than a dozen facilities. What began as a state-level cover-up expanded into a coordinated national pattern. We have heard testimony, authenticated sealed files, and released more than 370 names into The Archive Project."

She opened the folder slowly.

"But what we haven't talked about is who funded the silence."

She handed copies of the documents to the aides who passed them down the table.

"This is Crescent Holdings. It has appeared in at least three former state contracts under different names. What we believed were separate operations were in fact receiving money from the same trust. And that trust is directly connected to the man currently serving as chair of the National Child Protection Reform Alliance."

A low murmur moved through the room.

"David Marsh," she said. "The same man who has publicly praised our committee. The same man whose public donations support children's programming. The same man who helped shape the very federal protocols that allowed these name reassignments to remain hidden."

A tall man from the federal budget office raised a hand.

"Ms. Woods, these are serious accusations. Do you have financial records?"

"I do," Ava replied. "Attached in the appendix. You'll find four separate facility reports, each funded through layered subsidiaries. The original seed money can be traced back to Crescent Holdings."

Another member, a woman in glasses who had often remained neutral, looked over her copy.

"Is this information public?"

"No. Not yet. But it should be."

The room was silent again.

Selena cleared her throat.

"Thank you, Ms. Woods. The committee will now enter closed deliberation. You may return after we've concluded discussion."

Ava nodded once, gathered her things, and walked out without another word.

In the hallway, she sat alone on a bench, palms pressed against her knees. Her breath came slow, but her heart raced. Charity had told her to expect pushback. Nora had warned her that this step might shift allies into opponents.

But none of them had told her how lonely this moment would feel.

Thirty-seven minutes passed.

The chamber doors opened.

Selena stepped out and gestured.

Ava rose and followed her in.

All eyes turned to her.

Selena spoke formally.

"The committee has reviewed the submitted materials and confirmed the validity of the documentation. However, due to the sensitive nature of the accusations and the prominence of the individual involved, a vote was called."

Ava braced.

"The vote was to determine whether this matter would be escalated to the Department of Justice as an active inquiry, or whether it would be retained under internal review pending further discretion."

Selena paused.

"The vote was four to five. In favor of retaining."

Ava felt the breath leave her.

"So, we're burying it?"

Selena held up a hand. "No. But we're delaying it. There are members concerned that premature escalation could damage our credibility."

"Our credibility?" Ava repeated. "You mean your comfort."

Another committee member spoke. "This is bigger than all of us, Ms. Woods. A misstep here could unravel everything we've accomplished."

Ava's voice sharpened.

"Then maybe it should unravel."

The room tensed.

Selena met her eyes. "There is one more matter."

A paper was slid across the table.

It was a motion.

Proposal: Temporary Suspension of Committee Voting Powers for Ava Woods, Pending Oversight Review.

Ava stared at it.

No one would look her in the eye.

"Why?" she asked.

No answer came.

Just silence.

Selena said quietly, "It's not permanent. But the vote was submitted by members concerned about bias."

"Bias?" Ava asked. "Because I survived it?"

Selena didn't respond.

Ava stood.

"I won't fight you for a seat that was built on my story just to keep your rooms quiet. If you want to remove me, say it."

Another pause.

Selena finally said, "The vote is tomorrow morning."

Ava left without another word.

Back at The Crossing, Charity received the update in pieces: text messages, Nora's call, and a scanned copy of the committee's motion.

She stood at the edge of the construction site, the skeletal walls of the memorial behind her, the name bricks waiting in stacks.

Malcolm approached.

"She needs you."

"I know."

"She'll be fine."

Charity shook her head. "She doesn't need to be fine. She needs to be heard."

That night, Ava sat in her apartment in D.C., the pages from Crescent Holdings spread across her table. She stared at the same memo over and over, her father's handwriting, his last warning, and now the line she might not be allowed to cross.

A knock came at the door.

She opened it.

Charity stood there, windblown and tired.

Ava stepped aside.

They didn't speak for a moment.

Then Ava whispered, "I think they're going to vote me out."

Charity answered, "Then let them. But not before you say everything that needs to be said."

Ava sat down at the table.

"What if they shut the investigation down completely?"

"Then we don't need their table."

Ava looked at her. "We build our own."

That night, Ava wrote a letter.

She folded it into her notebook.

And the next morning, she entered the committee chamber with her head high.

Let them vote.

But let them do it after hearing her roar.

Act 3 – Chapter 38

Title: "The Vote"

The room was too still.

Ava sat at the long mahogany table, a folded piece of paper in her lap, her fingertips tracing the seam. Around her, the other committee members adjusted pens, avoided eye contact, and exchanged glances behind the veil of formality. The vote to suspend her seat was minutes away.

Selena Morales sat at the center. Neutral. Calm. But not without empathy.

"This session is now in order," she began, her voice even. "Before we move to the formal vote, Ms. Woods has requested time to speak. You may proceed."

Ava stood slowly.

She did not bring notes. She did not wear armor. She wore the gray suit her mother might have chosen for her, and the locket around her neck that had traveled from the ashes of a fire to the steps of the nation's most powerful rooms.

She looked out across the table.

"I don't need to defend my place here," she said, voice quiet but steady. "I earned it. I lived it. And I have paid for every word I speak with years of silence that was never mine to carry."

Someone shifted in their chair.

"I am not here to cause disruption. I am here because disruption was the only thing that gave me my name back."

A low murmur stirred in the gallery behind the glass.

Ava turned slightly toward them.

"My sister and I were children when the system decided our existence was too inconvenient. We were separated by design. Renamed by people who never saw us. And we were told that what we remembered could not be trusted."

She faced the committee again.

"I speak for the children who are still waiting to be found. And if my voice threatens your comfort, then maybe it's time we ask whose comfort this room was built to protect."

Her voice rose slightly.

"Do not confuse professionalism with passivity. I am calm, yes. But I am not quiet. I do not come with rage, I come with evidence. And that's what you're really afraid of."

Several heads turned away.

Ava continued.

"Crescent Holdings was not a footnote. It was the seed. It funded the policies we are now trying to fix. If you vote to ignore that, then this committee becomes just another piece of the machinery it was built to dismantle."

She paused. Looked down at the folded paper.

Then opened it.

It was her mother's letter, the one they had found behind the fireplace.

She read aloud.

"If they come for us, it is not because we did something wrong. It is because we did something right."

Ava folded the paper slowly, then placed it on the table.

"I am not here to make you comfortable," she said. "I am here to make us better."

She returned to her seat.

No applause.

No movement.

Just the stillness of truth, hanging like the final note of a hymn.

Selena nodded.

"The motion to suspend voting powers of Ms. Ava Woods, pending oversight review, is now open. Members, please mark your ballots."

Small slips were distributed.

The room filled with the soft sound of pens scratching paper.

Ava closed her eyes.

She thought of the fire.

She thought of the night her name was taken.

And the day she got it back.

The ballots were collected.

Selena opened them slowly, reading each one with a practiced hand. She did not betray the count until the last slip was opened.

Then she looked up.

"The final vote is five to four. Motion denied."

Ava's eyes opened.

The room stirred.

Then the surprise came.

One of the senior members: a man named Douglas Keene, who had never once supported her proposals, stood.

"I changed my vote," he said.

Murmurs erupted.

Selena raised her hand. "Mr. Keene, this is irregular"

"I don't care," he said, his voice stronger now. "She's right. We've been managing a narrative, not fixing a system. We were afraid of the implications. But fear isn't an excuse. If we're going to lead this reform, it needs to be led by the ones who lived it."

He turned to Ava.

"And Ms. Woods has lived it."

The press conference that followed was impromptu, but the energy around it was unmistakable.

Charity watched from Shady Grove, standing in the soon-to-be memorial courtyard, surrounded by newly poured cement and name bricks drying under the sun.

Ava stood behind the microphone with confidence and calm.

"No, I will not be stepping down from the committee," she said. "And yes, I will continue to push for transparency, even when it leads us to powerful people. Especially when it does."

A reporter called out, "Do you feel you're being targeted?"

Ava nodded. "Of course. But I am not afraid of being targeted. I'm afraid of what happens if I stop speaking."

Another hand rose. "What's next?"

Ava glanced at the note in her hand. Her mother's.

She smiled.

"What's next is justice."

That night, Ava returned home and found a package at her door.

No return label.

Inside was a copy of a juvenile case report.

Redacted, but partially legible.

And a sticky note.

"You were never supposed to find this. So, I left it where you would."
G.

Ava stared at the file.

And then she called Charity.

"We're not done," she said.

Charity answered, "We're just getting started."

Act 3 – Chapter 39

Title: "The Facility Without a Name"

The file was thin, but it carried weight.

Ava stared at the single line near the top of the page:

Subject transferred from Site 17C: Final Classification — "Non-reintegratable."

The term was clinical. Cold. Purposefully vague. But the stamp in the corner gave it away:

Crescent Holdings: Internal Routing Only.

Charity arrived at Ava's apartment an hour later. She didn't knock. She just stepped inside, coat still damp from the rain.

Ava handed her the file.

"Someone left it on my doorstep. No return label. Just this."

Charity scanned it, then paused on the notation at the bottom. Coordinates. Not an address. Not a city.

"Did you look it up?"

Ava nodded. "It leads to the mountains. Western Virginia. Deep interior. Closest road ends four miles from it."

"An old site?"

"Very."

Charity closed the file. "Then we go."

Two days later, they arrived in western Virginia.

The trees were thick and unyielding. The elevation changed subtly at first, then sharply. Malcolm had arranged a four-wheel-drive vehicle and insisted on traveling with them. Jasmine came too, seated in the back with a notebook on her lap and a pen she hadn't put down since they left the hotel.

No one spoke much as they climbed the unmarked path. Even the GPS gave up.

Eventually, the road disappeared, and they parked near a rusted gate half-buried in underbrush. Faded lettering on the steel read **"Stability Site 17C – Restricted Access."**

The silence was eerie.

Charity looked back. "Everyone ready?"

Ava nodded. Jasmine, too.

They crossed the gate line.

The facility emerged slowly from the forest, like a bruise under skin.

Gray concrete. Shuttered windows. Moss-covered signs. No roofline markings, no flags, no indication of what had once gone on here. The building had been forgotten by time and design.

They found the entrance unlocked.

Inside, the air was dry. The walls were still lined with bulletin boards, some with curling notices.

Ava read one aloud: "Quiet time protocol: 8 p.m. to 6 a.m. Any disruption will be noted."

Charity's stomach turned.

They explored in pairs.

Charity and Malcolm moved through what had once been offices, drawers empty, cabinets open, but scratches marked the walls where nameplates used to hang.

Ava and Jasmine entered a large hall with tiled floors and bolted-down furniture. The light came in at sharp angles. At the far end, a mural stretched across the wall, faded but legible.

"Stability is silence. Silence is strength."

Jasmine touched the wall lightly.

"I remember those words," she whispered.

Ava turned. "You were here?"

Jasmine nodded. "Before Thornhill. They moved me here for a 'quiet protocol.' I didn't speak for a year."

Ava stared at the mural. "How many others?"

"I don't know," Jasmine said. "They didn't use our names."

In the basement, they found the records room.

It had been stripped mostly bare, but one cabinet remained bolted into a corner. Locked.

Charity reached for the crowbar Malcolm had brought.

She pried it open.

Inside were rows of microfilm reels, each labeled with numbers. No names. Just codes.

Ava stepped forward and recognized the formatting.

"Same as the Archive. These are the original records."

Charity whispered, "They were hiding them underground."

They took the reels and loaded them into the portable scanner Jasmine had carried in her backpack. The screen flickered. Then text appeared:

"REED, J. – TRANSFER AUTHORIZED. PENDING BEHAVIORAL FINALITY."

"WESTFIELD, A. – RECLASSIFIED. NAME REDACTED."

Then, a third:

"WOODS, C. – RECORDS VOIDED. ENTRY BLOCKED."

Ava touched Charity's hand.

"They tried to erase you completely."

Charity stared at the screen.

"I wasn't supposed to survive. Not just the fire. The story."

Back at the hotel that night, they combed through the files.

Over seventy names, many of them matching early Archive entries, but several they had never seen.

One name made Charity freeze.

"Elijah Woods – Priority Disruption Tag."

Ava leaned in.

"They didn't just kill him. They flagged him."

Malcolm pulled a highlighted document from the reel.

"Look at this, meeting minutes. Internal memo between Crescent board members. Marsh's name is here."

Jasmine read the line aloud.

"Woods testimony must not reach federal channels. If needed, reclassify both daughters."

Charity said nothing.

She stood and walked to the window.

Then she whispered, "They planned it all."

The next morning, Ava submitted the reel scans to Nora and the legal team at The Crossing. Within an hour, the DOJ requested a secure briefing.

By noon, Senator Marsh's office had released a terse statement denying knowledge of any classified documents tied to Crescent Holdings.

By 3 p.m., reporters began knocking.

By evening, a federal investigation into Crescent Holdings was officially announced.

But it wasn't over.

Not yet.

That night, Ava and Charity sat on the hotel balcony, wrapped in silence.

"This feels different," Ava said. "Final."

Charity nodded. "Like a door closed."

Ava looked at her. "But we're still standing in the room."

Charity smiled faintly. "Then maybe it's time to build something beyond it."

The next day, they returned to Shady Grove.

Construction on the memorial was nearly complete. The bricks had been laid. The name wall was rising. And the garden was beginning to bloom.

Charity walked the path slowly.

She passed her mother's name.

Her father's.

And now, alongside them, a new name had been carved.

"All those they tried to unwrite."

She stood in front of the stone, tears in her eyes.

Ava stood beside her.

"Tomorrow," she said, "we open it to the world."

Charity whispered, "Let them come."

Act 3 – Chapter 40

Title: "The Wall of Names"

The morning was still.

Dew clung to the edges of flower petals and the corners of bricks. Sunlight passed through the trees like stained glass, casting fractured light on the newly poured stone path that wound through the heart of Shady Grove. The site that once held ashes now held names. Rows of them, carved into black granite, each letter cut with careful reverence.

The **Elijah and Leah Woods Center for Truth and Restoration** opened its gates at 9:00 a.m. sharp.

By 9:05, the courtyard was full.

They came from every direction, survivors, families, journalists, government officials, pastors, teachers, nurses, strangers. Some carried flowers. Others wore pins with their loved ones' names etched on them. Some carried silence, because words had never found them.

Ava stood near the edge of the courtyard, watching as rows of people filed in. Children ran their fingers along the engraved bricks. Elders knelt beside name markers. There were cameras, but they didn't lead. They followed.

Charity stood just beyond the gate, hands clasped behind her back. Her dress was a deep navy, simple, elegant. Her hair pinned back. Her eyes unreadable.

Jasmine stepped beside her. "They're ready."

Charity turned. "So are we."

Ava joined her at the center of the entrance where the microphone waited. Behind them stood the wall: twelve feet high, stretching from one side of the courtyard to the other. Names filled every inch.

A hush fell across the crowd.

Ava spoke first.

"When we first found each other again, my sister and I thought we were healing a family. Then we realized we were healing a history."

She looked toward the wall.

"This is not a memorial to the past. It's a promise to the future. That no child will be forgotten. That no voice will be erased."

She stepped back.

Charity took her place.

"My name is Charity Elaine Woods. I am the daughter of Elijah and Leah Woods. And I am a survivor of a system that tried to turn silence into safety."

She paused.

"Today, I walk this path not as a victim, but as a witness. I walk it with the names they tried to bury. And I walk it with you."

She turned slightly.

"Let the path begin."

One by one, the crowd began to move.

The path was a single winding arc, beginning at the name wall and circling the garden. At the end of the path was a low stone basin, where visitors were invited to place a small white stone in honor of the name they carried in their heart.

Charity led the first procession.

Ava at her side.

Jasmine beside her.

Malcolm and Nora following with survivors from The Crossing.

Each person paused at the wall.

Some whispered the names aloud.

Some touched the stone and simply cried.

Some placed photographs or folded pieces of paper in the flower beds lining the walkway.

A woman leaned in to Ava. "That's my brother's name. We never knew where he went. Thank you for finding him."

Ava nodded, unable to speak.

Charity paused near the center of the wall.

There, carved in perfect lines:

Elijah Marcus Woods
Leah Elaine Woods

Ava Denise Woods — Reclaimed
Charity Elaine Woods — Survived

She placed her hand gently on her father's name.

"You kept your promise," she whispered.

And then she kept hers.

By midday, the path was full of footprints and tears.

A choir from a local church stood near the back of the garden, humming softly. No microphones. No sheet music. Just harmony. Just breath.

Children sat on the benches beneath the oak trees, reading the laminated stories posted beside the wall—vignettes about the Woods family, about Jasmine's testimony, about the creation of The Archive Project.

Journalists walked quietly, cameras low.

The memorial asked something sacred of them.

To watch. Not perform.

Later in the day, Ava stood at the edge of the path, a small basket of white stones in her hands. One by one, children came forward to place a stone in the basin.

"Why do we put the stones here?" a boy asked her.

Ava knelt beside him. "Because memory weighs something. And now, it belongs here."

The boy placed the stone with care.

"So, people don't forget?"

Ava smiled. "Exactly."

At dusk, Charity walked the path one final time.

The sky had turned orange and violet, shadows stretching long. Lanterns had been lit around the wall, and soft music played through hidden speakers tucked into the garden hedges, strings and piano, no lyrics.

She paused at a small bench just beyond the final curve.

It had a plaque.

For those who returned. For those who never did.

Ava joined her moments later.

They sat in silence.

And then Ava said, "I got a call from the Department of Education. They want to include The Archive Project in the national curriculum."

Charity looked at her. "You're changing everything."

Ava shook her head. "We are."

They sat there until the last visitor had gone.

Until the music faded.

Until the names on the wall caught the last light of the sun.

Back inside the welcome center, the guest book overflowed with messages.

"I found my sister's name today."
"I brought my daughter to meet her aunt for the first time."
"I was erased. Today I was restored."

Charity read each one as she turned the pages.

Then she picked up the pen.

And wrote:

"Let no name be forgotten again. Not while we remember."
— *C. Woods*

Act 3 – Chapter 41

Title: "The Life You Choose"

Washington buzzed as usual. Horns in the distance. Phones ringing through glass partitions. Elevators humming their way up the steel spine of the federal building. But Ava stood still.

She stared out the window of her temporary office, the Capitol dome cutting the sky in half. The offer letter sat open on her desk behind her, white paper, heavy stock, official seal embossed in navy:

"The Department of Health and Human Services hereby extends to Ava Denise Woods an offer to serve as Director of National Youth Identity and Family Restoration Policy, effective immediately."

The position was historic.

Permanent.

High-profile.

And isolating.

Ava crossed her arms and kept her gaze on the horizon. She hadn't told Charity yet. Or Jasmine. Or Malcolm. The call had come in the night before, followed by the letter, hand-delivered by a senior aide this morning.

"You'll shape national protocols," the aide had said. "You'll speak for a generation."

But Ava wasn't sure she wanted to speak anymore. She wanted to breathe.

She spent the day walking the city.

Not on Capitol Hill.

Not on press routes.

She visited a small elementary school tucked between two brick apartment complexes. The principal had invited her weeks ago after reading an op-ed she published on the importance of child voice in policy reform.

The children didn't recognize her.

They asked her normal questions.

"What's your favorite color?"
"Do you like dinosaurs?"
"Are you a ballerina?"

Ava laughed, and the weight she carried loosened. She watched them draw pictures with reckless joy and raise their hands with the certainty that someone would answer.

When she left, the principal walked her to the curb.

"They don't know your story," she said. "They just know your presence made them feel safe."

Ava smiled softly. "That's more than enough."

That evening, she boarded the train to Shady Grove.

She didn't tell anyone she was coming. She needed time to think without counsel, without headlines. The train rocked gently beneath her. She leaned her head against the window and let the trees blur past.

When she arrived, the town smelled like wood smoke and summer.

The Crossing's shuttle picked her up without fanfare. She rode in the back, hoodie up, face turned away from the driver's glance.

When she stepped onto the grounds of the memorial, it was late.

The courtyard was empty.

Lanterns glowed in warm pools of light along the path. The name wall stood still and silent, like it had always been there. Ava walked slowly, heels echoing across the stone.

She found Charity inside the archive wing.

Her sister stood over a display table, reviewing new digital submissions to The Archive. Charity looked up and smiled the moment she saw her.

"You came home," she said.

Ava nodded. "I needed to."

They embraced without words. It was enough.

Later that night, they sat on the bench in the garden, the same one from the dedication.

Charity passed her a cup of hot tea.

"You've been quiet," she said gently.

Ava nodded. "They offered me a permanent post. National policy director."

Charity took a breath. "That's a big title."

Ava smiled faintly. "It comes with a corner office and a security detail."

"And?"

"And... I don't know if it comes with a life."

Charity turned to her. "You've already changed the country. But changing a system doesn't mean you have to lose yourself in it."

Ava looked toward the wall.

"I keep thinking about Mama. About the way she protected us—not with power, but with words. With letters. With lullabies. I don't want to become someone who only lives through legislation."

Charity reached for her hand.

"Then don't. Build something smaller. Something that lasts."

Ava let the silence settle between them.

"I want a home," she said at last. "I want to wake up and plant something. I want to teach. I want to love someone without needing to prepare a statement about it."

Charity smiled. "Then the answer's already here."

Ava looked down at her lap. "Will they be disappointed in me?"

Charity squeezed her hand. "Only if you stop being honest. And you never have."

The next morning, Ava stood at the lectern inside The Crossing's media room. A dozen local reporters and national correspondents waited with microphones ready.

Charity sat off to the side.

Nora stood in the back.

Malcolm watched with quiet pride.

Ava adjusted the microphone.

"I have made my decision regarding the federal appointment," she began, her voice calm. "It is an honor I never imagined. And I thank those who saw value in my voice. But I am declining the role."

Murmurs rippled across the room.

"I believe national change begins in the smallest places, in memory, in family, in one child hearing their name spoken aloud again. I will continue this work. But not in a corner office. In classrooms. In gardens. In courtrooms. In homes."

She stepped back.

Reporters scrambled to reframe their questions.

But Ava had already walked away.

That evening, she stood beneath the stars outside the welcome center.

Jasmine joined her, wrapping a shawl around her shoulders.

"I thought you'd take it," she said.

Ava smiled. "So did I."

"Are you sure?"

"Yes," Ava whispered. "Because I've never felt freer."

Jasmine looked up at the sky.

"I've started writing again."

Ava turned. "Really?"

"Poems. About names. About silence."

"Will you let me read one?"

"Soon."

They stood side by side.

And the future no longer looked like a stage or a platform.

It looked like a life.

Chapter 42

Title: "The Last Testimony"

The courtroom was filled before sunrise.

Media crews lined the sidewalk outside, their lenses fogging in the morning air. Inside, every seat was taken, by survivors, families, public officials who had once stayed silent. The weight of the moment pressed into the walls. There was no spectacle. Just presence.

Charity sat in the front row, wearing a black dress and her mother's silver pendant. Her hands were calm. Her eyes were still. Ava sat beside her, shoulders square, expression unreadable.

On the other side of the courtroom, Dr. Althea Randall was led in under federal custody.

She wore no badge. No title.

Only plain gray fabric and the restraint of quiet consequence.

Judge Bradford entered and called the session to order.

"This hearing marks the formal conclusion of *United States v. Carlisle et al.*, with the sentencing and public record declaration of all findings, sealed and unsealed."

A silence fell so complete it rang like sound.

A clerk stood and read the charges aloud.

Fraud.

Conspiracy to obstruct justice.

Abuse of federal funding.

Coercion of identity reassignment in minors.

When the list concluded, Dr. Randall stood at the judge's instruction.

"Dr. Randall," Judge Bradford said, "you were granted an opportunity to make a final statement. You may speak now."

Randall stepped to the microphone slowly.

Her voice was thinner than anyone remembered.

"I did what I thought was necessary," she said. "I followed protocols designed to protect the state from chaos. I see now that what we considered order was merely oppression with clean handwriting."

She paused, voice trembling.

"I don't ask for forgiveness. I ask only that the children who were hurt, those who survived, know that their defiance saved others."

She sat.

No applause.

No reaction.

Only stillness.

Judge Bradford read the sentence without hesitation.

"Althea Randall is hereby sentenced to twenty-five years in federal prison, with no possibility of parole, and is barred from ever again holding a government, academic, or advisory role tied to public welfare."

She closed the file.

"And now," the judge continued, "with the court's permission, we recognize a final piece of testimony entered into the record by the late Judge Elijah Woods. His daughter, Charity Elaine Woods, has been granted authority to read it aloud."

A wave passed through the courtroom.

Charity stood slowly and approached the microphone.

She unfolded the aged, brittle paper with reverence.

She did not look up until she began to speak.

"To whomever finds these words, know this, The system I served no longer reflects the justice I believed in. The children I tried to protect have been reduced to numbers. Those in power have stopped listening. I am leaving this record behind not as a warning, but as a compass."

"My daughters are alive. If I do not live to see them whole again, let the record show I never stopped trying. Let the record show their names."

"Ava Denise Woods.
Charity Elaine Woods."

Charity's voice shook, but she did not pause.

"They were never lost. They were never invisible. They were made that way by design."

She looked up at the courtroom.

"And now they have been made visible by choice."

She folded the paper slowly.

And whispered, "We're here, Daddy."

Outside, the press mobbed the steps.

But Ava and Charity didn't stay for statements.

They walked side by side through the crowd, unbothered by the flashes and voices. Justice was not in the camera clicks. It had been spoken. And it would remain.

At the base of the courthouse steps, Jasmine waited.

She handed each of them a small white stone.

"For your father," she said.

They placed them side by side on the courthouse lawn.

Two stones.

Two daughters.

One truth.

That evening, the headlines broke:

"Randall Sentenced. Woods Testimony Echoes Across Nation."

"Final Pages of Justice Read by Surviving Daughter."
"'Let the Record Show': A New Chapter Begins."

The nation took notice.

But Charity sat alone in her office at The Crossing, lights low, the copy of her father's letter now framed beside her desk.

She reached for her journal.

She wrote five words:

"He saw us. We rose."

She closed the book and turned off the light.

Act 3 – Chapter 43

Title: "The Crossing Reborn"

Six months passed.

In that time, The Crossing transformed.

What once occupied a single brownstone in lower Manhattan now echoed across the country. Twelve satellite chapters had launched in major cities. Each was modeled after the original: survivor-led, memory-centered, and community-driven.

Charity stood on the balcony of the new flagship location in Atlanta, Georgia, overlooking a gathering of nearly two hundred survivors and families. Below her, white tents billowed in the wind. Tables of archived documents and visual exhibits wrapped around the courtyard. Young people, many no older than she had been when her name was first taken, now stood at the forefront, leading sessions, guiding new arrivals, and naming what had never been spoken aloud before.

Jasmine stood at the center of it all.

She wore a soft maroon blazer, her natural curls pulled back, her voice calm and steady as she greeted a small group of teen girls just arriving from a youth housing program in Tennessee.

Charity watched her with quiet pride.

Jasmine no longer flinched at microphones. No longer looked down when telling her story. She had learned not just to speak, but to teach.

Malcolm stepped onto the balcony beside her.

"She's really stepping into it," he said.

"She is," Charity replied.

"And you're stepping back."

Charity didn't answer right away.

Instead, she leaned against the railing, the wind brushing through her coat.

"I've told the story," she finally said. "I've walked the fire. Now it's time to build something steadier."

Malcolm looked at her, then reached into his coat pocket and pulled out a small, folded envelope.

"What's this?" she asked.

"Jasmine wrote it. She asked me to hold onto it until today."

Charity opened it gently.

The note was handwritten, neat, and simple.

**"You found my voice.
Now I'll use it to find others."**

— Jasmine

Charity folded the note slowly and placed it in her pocket.

She didn't need to say a word.

That afternoon, they held a panel on post-trauma leadership. Jasmine moderated. Ava joined virtually from North Carolina, her background a wall of bookshelves and a wide-open window looking out on the woods behind her home.

During the Q&A, a young woman raised her hand.

She looked barely twenty, her voice cautious.

"What if I don't want to lead? What if I just want to be, okay?"

The room hushed.

Jasmine didn't hesitate.

"Then being okay is your revolution," she said. "We're not all meant to carry the microphone. Some of us are meant to heal quietly. And that is just as sacred."

Ava added, "Truth doesn't require an audience. It just requires a witness."

The young woman nodded slowly, tears in her eyes.

And Charity understood.

They were no longer only telling their story.

They were giving others permission to live their own.

Later, in the quiet of the conference room, Charity met with the founding chapter leads from Los Angeles, Chicago, Dallas, and Detroit.

They discussed budget projections, staffing growth, and survivor housing expansion.

Then someone asked, "Where do you see yourself in five years, Ms. Woods?"

Charity smiled.

"Planting things."

They laughed gently.

"No seriously," one said.

Charity leaned back in her chair.

"I see myself on the board. Advising. Writing. Maybe teaching again. But not running the day-to-day. This has to live beyond me."

They all nodded, quietly moved.

Because that was leadership too, knowing when to stand back so others could stand tall.

That night, Charity and Jasmine walked the campus garden together. The Atlanta center had replicated the same open-air courtyard as the Shady Grove memorial, complete with a name wall, memory bricks, and a central basin for white stones.

"I had no idea it could be like this," Jasmine said.

Charity looked up at the stars. "Neither did I. But maybe that's the point."

Jasmine turned. "You're really going to step away?"

Charity nodded. "Not gone. Just... quieter."

Jasmine took a breath.

"Then I'm ready."

They paused in front of the wall.

A new name had just been added:

Jasmine Imani Pierce — Advocate. Survivor. Voice Unbroken.

Jasmine touched the engraving, her eyes glassy.

Then she turned to Charity and whispered, "Thank you for staying until I could see myself."

Charity smiled. "Now go help someone else see."

In New York, the original Crossing brownstone remained intact.

Not as headquarters.

As a museum.

A quiet one. No ticketing. No fanfare. Just rooms filled with names, letters, documents, audio clips. A timeline of truth.

Inside the entrance, framed in wood and glass, hung a quote from Elijah Woods:

"Justice is not the sound of a gavel. It is the sound of a child remembering their own name."

People came from all over.

They walked the halls.

They wrote their names in the guestbook.

Some signed with the name they were given.

Others with the one they had reclaimed.

All of them were seen.

Charity returned to Shady Grove two weeks later.

She walked the garden barefoot, the soil still soft from rain.

Children from the local school had begun tending the garden beds. Letters from visitors hung on a nearby bulletin board. A swing had been installed beneath the old oak tree.

She sat on the bench, the locket around her neck, and breathed in the scent of wild rosemary and roses.

The war was not over.

But the fire no longer had the last word.

And that, she knew, was enough for now.

Chapter 44

Title: "A Name for Every Star"

The night was clear.

The air at Shady Grove held the kind of hush that came only when something sacred was about to happen. Hundreds of folding chairs had been arranged beneath the oak trees, each one filled with survivors, family members, supporters, and quiet witnesses to the long road of justice.

Overhead, string lights shimmered between the branches like constellations. Children passed through the aisles carrying candles in glass jars, setting them gently on the perimeter of the name wall. Their faces glowed in the soft light.

It was the official national opening of the **Elijah and Leah Woods Center for Truth and Restoration**.

A moment that had taken decades to arrive.

Charity stood backstage beneath a canopy tent, reviewing the final program. Her speech was ready, but she wouldn't be the one to open the ceremony.

That honor belonged to Jasmine.

At 7:00 p.m. sharp, Jasmine stepped to the stage. She didn't use a script. She didn't read a note. She simply stood with the stillness of someone who had learned how to carry the weight of her story.

"This memorial is not made of stone," she began. "It's made of names. Names that were taken, hidden, rewritten, and in some cases, nearly lost. Tonight, we speak them aloud."

She stepped back.

And the music began.

A choir of thirty voices rose from the right side of the lawn, humming an original composition, a blend of gospel tones and Appalachian roots. No lyrics. Just longing and strength wrapped in melody.

One by one, names were read aloud by survivors who had traveled from every corner of the country.

Some paused to whisper the names.

Some cried as they read their own.

Some read two names, one they had been given, and the one they had reclaimed.

When the last name echoed into the stars, Jasmine returned to the microphone.

"We were not forgotten," she said. "We were found."

Charity stepped up next.

The crowd hushed once again.

She carried a single envelope in her hand.

Before she spoke, she turned toward the memorial wall, where Ava's name was etched among the restored identities.

AVA DENISE WOODS — Remembered. Remembering.

Charity looked out over the sea of candles and faces.

"My sister could not be here tonight," she said gently. "But she sent something."

She held up the letter.

"It's not just for me. It's for all of you."

She unfolded the page and began to read.

"To those who came before me
To those who were silenced
To those who remember
And to those who one day will:

There is no perfect ending for stories like ours.
There is only truth. And truth is enough.
Truth keeps breathing after the fire.
Truth finds you when your name has been taken.
Truth sounds like a girl in a locked room,
whispering her real name to herself so she doesn't forget.
It sounds like a knock on the door from someone you thought was lost.
It sounds like the word 'home' being spoken for the first time without fear."

"If you are reading this, or hearing it, or standing beneath these stars and wondering what comes next, I want you to know this
You do not have to become famous to be free.
You do not have to carry everyone else's pain to

prove that you survived.
You only have to remember that your name matters.
And that no one, not a judge, or a system, or a piece of paper, can tell you who you are."

"I am Ava Denise Woods.
I was lost.
I was renamed.
I was found."

"And if you are standing here,
then you have been found too."

"I leave this not as a goodbye,
but as a beginning.
A name for every star.
A name for every voice.
A name for you."

— Ava

The silence after the reading was full and sacred.

Charity stood still for a moment, letter lowered, hands trembling but steady. The people did not speak. They let the words settle in the air like ash becoming light.

Then a single voice called out from the crowd.

"I remember."

Then another.

"I remember."

Then dozens more.

"I remember."

"I remember."

"I remember."

And the garden was filled with the only sound that mattered.

Memory.

Later, the choir began to sing again.

Jasmine and Charity stood at the basin and invited attendees to place a white stone in the water—each one representing a life restored, a truth reclaimed.

The pool filled slowly.

But completely.

As the stars wheeled above them, Charity looked toward the path lined with bricks. The names glowed faintly in the light.

She knew this was not the end of the fight.

But it was the end of the forgetting.

And that, finally, was enough.

Epilogue

Title: "The Sky Still Holds Us"
Seven Years Later

The sky above Shady Grove was soft with morning light, the kind of pale gold that made everything look newly made. A breeze moved gently through the wildflowers planted beside the courtyard stones, scattering petals like prayers over the path.

The memorial stood exactly as it had been built. Still. Whole. Eternal.

Inside the archive building, a group of children sat cross-legged on the polished floor, listening to a volunteer read aloud from a binder labeled **"Voices from The Archive."**

Today's voice was Ava Woods.

The children listened in silence as the story unfolded, not of the trauma, but of the return. Of the naming. Of the remembering. They were too young to know the full weight of what had come before, but they felt the importance in the hush of the room, in the way the adult reading paused before certain words.

Outside, Charity walked the path alone.

She no longer worked day to day at The Crossing. She had passed the leadership to a council of survivors and educators, young and fiercely clear-eyed. Jasmine had become Executive Director two years ago. Under her leadership, The Crossing had tripled its reach, established a trauma-informed certification program for youth facilities, and opened two international chapters.

Charity had moved to a quiet cottage just past the edge of town.

She taught literature at the local college.

Planted wild things in her garden.

And woke up every morning without fear.

Her phone buzzed in her pocket.

A message from Ava.

"Sent you something. Should arrive today. Also, don't forget to walk barefoot in the grass like Mama told us."

Charity smiled. Then looked up and saw the delivery van near the memorial's front office.

She walked over, thanked the courier, and carried the package to the garden bench beneath the oak.

Inside the box was a journal.

Hand-bound.

On the first page was Ava's handwriting.

"To Charity—The first voice I heard when I came home."

Each page held letters from survivors.

Stories of names reclaimed.

Photos of families reunited.

Drawings from children who would never be renamed again.

And at the end, a single quote:

**"We were not meant to be legends.
We were meant to be whole."**

Charity closed the journal, held it against her chest, and leaned back into the bench.

She let the sun warm her face.

She let the silence hold her.

Far away, on a different coast, Ava stood before a group of high school seniors. She had agreed to speak at one school per year, only one. No camera crews. No formal engagements. Just stories.

She finished reading an excerpt from her father's letter, folded it carefully, and stepped aside.

A girl with tightly braided hair raised her hand.

"What happened after?"

Ava smiled.

"We lived."

The girl blinked. "That's it?"

"That's everything."

The students clapped softly.

And Ava walked outside, her steps steady.

She had a train to catch.

Tomorrow, she would visit a new garden being built at a youth center in Baltimore. The kids had named it after Jasmine.

She would bring stones from Shady Grove.

Back at the original memorial, Jasmine stood beneath the name wall, reading from a clipboard. Two interns followed her, listening carefully as she outlined plans for the new digital exhibit, one that would allow visitors to hear survivor recordings as they walked the path.

She was taller now.

Still soft-spoken, but never unsure.

She no longer wrote only for herself.

Her first poetry collection had been published last year.

It was called **"Named."**

It was already being taught in classrooms.

One poem had been etched into the final stone added to the basin:

**"I said my name,
and the silence broke."**

As dusk fell, Charity returned to her cottage, where the porch light flickered on with a soft hum. She set the journal down beside her reading chair, opened the windows, and turned on the kettle.

Outside, the wind moved gently through the trees.

Inside, she sat down, opened her favorite worn book, and read the line her mother had once underlined in red:

"The world breaks everyone, and afterward, many are strong at the broken places."

She folded the page softly and whispered, "Thank you."

To no one.

To everyone.

Later that night, a young girl walked the path of names alone.

She had never known her mother.

But she knew her name now.

It was on the wall.

She knelt beside it, traced the letters with her fingers, then placed a white stone in the basin.

She whispered her own name aloud, just once.

And then walked into the night.

Whole.

The End

www.ingramcontent.com/pod-product-compliance
Lightning Source LLC
LaVergne TN
LVHW041658060526
838201LV00043B/479